Of Song and Water

ADVANCE PRAISE

Of Song and Water is one of the most moving and vulnerable books I have ever read. Rhonda's work is personal and passionate. The spiritual growth and musical journey are so tightly woven together that the two aspects become inseparable—introspective, honest, and intense. Rhonda has traveled a difficult but rewarding path. Her willingness to share that journey is impactful and at times overwhelming, being clearly unafraid to take the proverbial path less traveled that led to self-discovery and an inseparable personal relationship to the music she loves. There is never a sense of self-pity or "poor me," only a willingness to learn from life's experiences, good or bad, demonstrating a drive to build the best possible life. *Of Song and Water* inspires everyone to continue the search knowing full well that "better" is always attainable.

Eugene Migliaro Corporon
Regents Professor of Music
Director of Wind Studies
College of Music
University of North Texas

Artistic Director/Conductor
North Texas Wind Symphony

RHONDA L. MUCKERMAN

OF SONG
AND
WATER

A Journey to Hope
and Healing Conducted
Through Music
and Nature

NEW YORK

LONDON • NASHVILLE • MELBOURNE • VANCOUVER

Of Song and Water

A Journey to Hope and Healing Conducted Through Music and Nature

Published in New York, New York, by Morgan James Publishing. Morgan James is a trademark of Morgan James, LLC. www.MorganJamesPublishing.com

Proudly distributed by Ingram Publisher Services.

Morgan James BOGO™

A **FREE** ebook edition is available for you or a friend with the purchase of this print book.

CLEARLY SIGN YOUR NAME ABOVE

Instructions to claim your free ebook edition:
1. Visit MorganJamesBOGO.com
2. Sign your name CLEARLY in the space above
3. Complete the form and submit a photo of this entire page
4. You or your friend can download the ebook to your preferred device

ISBN 9781631956775 paperback
ISBN 9781631956782 ebook
Library of Congress Control Number: 2021940454

Cover Design by:
Megan Dillon
megan@creativeninjadesigns.com

Interior Design by:
Christopher Kirk
www.GFSstudio.com

Morgan James is a proud partner of Habitat for Humanity Peninsula and Greater Williamsburg. Partners in building since 2006.

Get involved today! Visit MorganJamesPublishing.com/giving-back

To the Queen of the Waters,
and to the One from whom all Song originates.

TABLE OF CONTENTS

ACKNOWLEDGMENTS ix

CHAPTER ONE **REQUIEM**. 1
CHAPTER TWO **PREPARATORY BEAT**. 5
CHAPTER THREE **DOWN-BEAT**. 11
CHAPTER FOUR **SONG** 15
CHAPTER FIVE **KICK-STEP**. 19
CHAPTER SIX **VASSAR** 25
CHAPTER SEVEN **CINCINNATI** 29
CHAPTER EIGHT **WESTWARD FLIGHT** 37
CHAPTER NINE **SEATTLE RAINS**. 41
CHAPTER TEN **SWEAT**. 45
CHAPTER ELEVEN **SPIRIT** 53
CHAPTER TWELVE **THE VOICE**. 61

CHAPTER THIRTEEN **PORT ORFORD** 67
CHAPTER FOURTEEN **NEVADA SONG**. 71
CHAPTER FIFTEEN **NATIVE FLUTE** 75
CHAPTER SIXTEEN **THE WATERS WITHIN** 79
CHAPTER SEVENTEEN **AN OLD HORSE** 83
CHAPTER EIGHTEEN **BLACK CANYON** 91
CHAPTER NINETEEN **MOVE TO TELLURIDE**. 97
CHAPTER TWENTY **PETER**. 101
CHAPTER TWENTY-ONE **MOUNTAIN MUSIC** 107
CHAPTER TWENTY-TWO **MOTHERHOOD**. 111
CHAPTER TWENTY-THREE
                    A GROWING DARKNESS 115
CHAPTER TWENTY-FOUR **ELIOT** 119
CHAPTER TWENTY-FIVE **NORWOOD** 125
CHAPTER TWENTY-SIX **SAN MIGUEL** 131
CHAPTER TWENTY-SEVEN
                    ILLNESS AND DEATH. 137
CHAPTER TWENTY-EIGHT **DROWNING**. 143
CHAPTER TWENTY-NINE **MACHU PICCHU**. 149
CHAPTER THIRTY **ROAD TRIP** 155
CHAPTER THIRTY-ONE **MYSTIC RIVER**. 159
CHAPTER THIRTY-TWO **COZUMEL** 163
CHAPTER THIRTY-THREE **A SHIP TURNS**. 171
CHAPTER THIRTY-FOUR **PEARLS** 173
CHAPTER THIRTY-FIVE **JUNCTION CREEK** 177
CHAPTER THIRTY-SIX **A STREAM OF SONG** 185

ABOUT THE AUTHOR. 191

ACKNOWLEDGMENTS

To my parents, Faye and Louis, who picked me up at every band rehearsal, drove me to every lesson, and listened to endless scales and etudes.

To my husband, Peter, who is my greatest companion in life.

To my daughter, Ellen. Your voice is my favorite of all!

To Eliot, may you be at peace wherever you are.

To my friends, Peter and Michelle, who gave me the idea to write this book and provided some much-needed writing advice early in the process.

To Christine Odle for your support in connecting me with Morgan James Publishing.

To the Morgan James Publishing family, including David Hancock, Jim Howard, and Emily Madison for giving me the opportunity and necessary support to bring this book out into the world.

To my editor, Aubrey Kosa, who helped me to see myself as a real writer and patiently dredged through all my dashes.

To all of the musicians whom I have the honor to conduct. You are my teachers.

CHAPTER ONE

REQUIEM

"Dear Lord, I wander here below, glory hallelujah!
I sing to you that I may know, glory hallelujah!
Have I a seat in Paradise? Glory hallelujah!
Is there a Love that never dies? Glory hallelujah!
I have some friends before me gone, glory hallelujah.
But I'm resolved to travel on, glory hallelujah.
I vow that I'll remember them, glory hallelujah.
Their memory a requiem, glory hallelujah!"

~ from "Hymnody of Earth," Malcolm Dalglish

I sing the opening lines to the packed church, surrounded by dearly loved community members, their faces reflecting sadness, uncertainty. My tenor voice, low for a woman's vocal range, implores to the rafters and beyond. By the third line of the song, my friend Dalen harmonizes solemnly from his place in the top row of the bass section, his eyebrows lifted and head tilted.

The remaining voices of the thirty-member Chorale join on "I have some friends before me gone," our voices trembling, exposing the rawness of our hearts. I am grateful for their support, for my voice cracks and goes silent for a few beats before I can rejoin them for "I vow that I'll remember them, glory hallelujah."

I turn toward the members of the Telluride Choral Society, arms raised to conduct the simple cut-time meter, swooping down and up. I notice my left arm, floating out to the side, dismembered, the distance growing between my heart and hand—a reflection of the moment our family is passing through, having gone from four of us to only three.

Ten days earlier, we found our twenty-five-year-old son, Eliot, dead from a drug overdose. Lying on his couch, one leg hanging out from under the blanket that partially covered his face. A detritus of empty Dust-Off compressed air cans—which we soon learned cause a "high" similar to that of heroin—littered the coffee table and floor nearby. There were groceries on the kitchen island, not yet put away, and appointments written on his calendar—evidence of his unintentional asphyxiation.

It happened on the day of the final dress rehearsal for our annual spring concert. My friends and board members swam through an ocean of details, rescheduling the concert, crossing out the original date on the posters around our small, mountain town with Sharpie markers, while my family drowned.

Now we emerge from a week and a half of casseroles, phone calls, and visits. My husband, Peter, stands in the bass section of the choir, his eyes blue and steady and sorrowful, and our teenage daughter, Ellen, sits in the pews with an audience comprised of long-time friends, family—those who knew us for some twenty years. My breath is shallow, my vision fuzzy, the shock of grief and the sudden weight of having to hold my family together sweating out through my pores. As the voices of my singers fill me, hold me up, I ask myself, "How will I conduct without my left arm? How will I conduct my music, my life?"

CHAPTER TWO

PREPARATORY BEAT

I was raised in Clifton, NJ, with its humid summers, our above-ground pool shimmering endlessly blue in the backyard. My early childhood was shaped by the rising and falling hum of cicadas, an ocean of sound, wild and unrestrained, the first music I knew. Later I was formed by the sounds of the flute section in school concert bands, warm tones of woodwinds and brass, and the musty odor of the instrument storage rooms where we hurriedly jammed our instruments on too-small shelves before rushing to our next class. The just-rehearsed melodies and scales trailed after us through the hallways.

My interest in musical instruments began with an old "player" piano in my babysitter's basement when I was five years old. It sat opposite a shiny, blinking pinball machine. While my friends ran to the pinball machine, flipping levers gleefully, I approached the piano, drawn to the black notes on the yellowed pages, the wooden bench creaking beneath me as I touched the keys for the first time. Slightly out of tune, the keys rang nevertheless, an alarm clock of joy and remembrance.

Since we did not have a piano in our home, my parents purchased electric Hammond organs that grew with my talent, octave by octave, year by year. The parade of instruments continued throughout my childhood with my father's Hohner harmonica at age seven and an acoustic guitar that I purchased for twenty dollars from the above-mentioned babysitter. Each one was a vessel, shaping me with a new vibration.

As a fourth-grader, I discovered how to play hundreds of songs on a five-dollar "flutophone" that my grandmother, Victoria, insisted the school allow me to keep at the end of the school year. I still have the letter she wrote to the principal, her graceful cursive citing my love for music and need to continue playing; she even enclosed a five-dollar bill in the envelope to pay for the instrument. I brought her note to school, and within a few hours, the custodian led me down to the basement where all of the flutophones from all of the fourth-graders were spread out on tables, awaiting sterilization before being stored away for the summer. I picked mine out—I had written my name on the inside of the case in indelible magic marker, marking it from day one—and brought it home, along with the five-dollar bill the principal refused to accept.

The flute became my "major" instrument later on, and as a teenager, I practiced daily in my parents' bedroom. One evening, as I reeled through my scales, Grandmother Victoria rocked in the chair nearby. Her head nodded beneath a cap of dyed red hair, eyes closed in concentration, a sentinel who guarded the sanctity of my musical path.

"Play with more feeling!" she implored, gesticulating broadly, her Italian heritage filling the corner of the room.

I grimaced and rolled my eyes, resistant in my thirteen-year-old arrogance. As a self-conscious teenager, I couldn't connect with her unrelenting advice that I play with "more feeling."

But only a couple of years later, I was awakening to the feelings my grandmother had demanded of me in my after-school symphonic band rehearsals. A nerdy kid, just out of braces, with wavy brown hair that refused to be blow-dried into the coveted "feathers" of the early eighties, I found myself smiling shyly during our rehearsals, my heart leaping at the dramatic flourishes of Vaughan Williams and melting at Grainger's "Irish Tune from County Derry." The music of Holst's "First Suite" in E-flat transported me to another place inside myself and accompanied our band across the ocean to the Harrogate Music Festival in England where we performed for international audiences. Like an old friend, its song was familiar and compassionate, bringing me a sense of clarity and peace, a depth of feeling that simply said, "It's okay. This is your home, your place in life."

Mr. Morgan was my high school band director, and I was equally terrified and mystified by him. He showed his love for us by the repertoire with which he stuffed our black leatherette folders. No "macaroni and cheese" music for us—only the British Band classics and fine orchestral transcriptions would do!

He was well over six feet tall, large in both stature and energy. On one particular autumn day, our marching band stood at attention in a loose formation on the practice field, sweating and out of breath, the dry grass flattened beneath us. He softly muttered a profanity, then proceeded to run at us, full speed, in an effort to bulldoze us into the right positions. A few kids in the trumpet section who weren't paying attention to his barreling form were comically knocked off their feet like cartoon characters, but the rest of us hopped out of his path. The piccolo section was safe, smug with our tiny instruments jammed into our back pockets during drill practice. Years later, I would remember the ease of a tiny instrument with fondness and appreciation when helping my daughter schlep her bass guitars and amplifiers.

When in tune, the piccolo section added a bright shimmer to the overall sound of the showband, sparkling through the repertoire of classical pieces, jazz, marches, and seventies rock hits while we high-stepped and swaggered our way to local fame. Everyone stayed in the stands during half-time in Clifton, NJ— our shows were much more interesting than the football game.

How I loved those late afternoon rehearsals. The sky darkened around us, whether outside on the football field or inside the cramped band room, while my mother waited in the car to bring me home. After riding this trajectory for years, I decided to major in music therapy, a form of rehabilitation using music as a vehicle for healing. Michigan State University (MSU) had developed the first program in the United States, so I set my sights on attending after I finished high school. This was in the early eighties—pre-internet—so I had only a brochure from a school roughly 600 miles away from home. On its cover, the Red Cedar River flowed through campus, juniper and maple trees lining its banks. In my mind, I had already set sail.

Not wanting to waste any time, I sent off my only college application to MSU in September of my senior year. I prepared the required audition tape and after recording the required scales and solo pieces, I threw in one more piece: Fantaisie Hongroise by Franz Doppler, which I was wild about at the time. A highly ornamented melody in D minor, it is filled with romantic flourishes and tempo changes until it finally closes with a big, expressive finish. I ventured outside the box of what was required, hoping that the audition faculty would get a better sense of who I was. Rather than the live audition that many Michiganders would experience, the committee would only have a cassette tape mailed in a plain envelope from New Jersey by which to judge me.

One month later, I received a response from MSU. My parents perched the unopened letter on the kitchen table for me to open after an early Saturday morning marching band rehearsal. The first words read, "Congratulations, you are a Spartan!" in green and white—the team colors of MSU. My mom and I celebrated in our traditional fashion by going to the mall and raiding the discount racks. I was on my way!

Upon hearing the news of my acceptance, Mr. Morgan gave me the opportunity to conduct the marching band during the national anthem at the final home football game of my senior year. He had given me some rudimentary coaching about how to conduct in a three-beat pattern—down, out, up—and how to throw a few cues to the percussion section so that the cymbals would crash at the right time. We rehearsed a couple of times during the week, and on game day, I climbed the tall ladder in my heavy woolen uniform, complete with a red cape and what I called a buffalo hat (a furry, tall hat in which you could stow a raincoat if needed on a damp, November day).

Donning white, cotton gloves, I brought my hands up, signaling the instrumentalists to raise their horns in a quick "whoosh" of readiness. Two preparatory beats later, the entire band entered, following my tempo. The wall of sound passed through me and across the field to the people in the grandstands, the powerful vibrations of brass, percussion, and shimmering cymbals as my arms moved down, out, and up, my left hand above my head cueing the flashing cymbals, my heart beating hard in my chest—an architecture of celebration.

CHAPTER THREE

DOWNBEAT

I n the fall of 1982, I entered MSU in East Lansing, Michigan as a music therapy major. Far from home in a new landscape, surrounded by green fields and the faint stench of cattle farms—MSU had a long tradition of being an agricultural university—I relished the opportunity to start over, not knowing a single person. I made fast friends in those early days and happily settled into a new routine, navigating my way around the 10,000-acre campus, frequently lost, with a goofy smile on my face.

As a freshman, it was rare to earn a spot in the Symphony Band at MSU, but after fall auditions, I managed to place near the bottom of the flute section. I was thrilled to have the chance to play with some serious musicians, many of whom were upperclassmen.

On the very first day of rehearsal I entered the band room, an old rehearsal room with high ceilings and draped walls, in which I would spend hundreds of hours in the years to come. We warmed up and thumbed through the music in our folders. The conductor of the Symphony Band came in the standard uniform of black turtleneck and slacks and ascended the podium. He appraised us, dark eyes gleaming, with a mysterious smile on his face and said, "Take a look at the person next to you." Turning to the young woman next to me, also a freshman, I smiled.

"You are looking at a really talented person," he stated simply, nodding.

The glow of the late afternoon sun slanted through the high windows as the warmth of his compliment spread through us, blessed, having arrived here together. Our conductor indicated the piece, "Homage," with which we would begin rehearsal. Placing it on our stands, instruments poised, we awaited his downbeat to begin. When it arrived with a flourish, the band entered with it, but I was stunned and could not do anything. I could only stare at the beauty of his conducting, speechless, my mouth hanging open, for I had never seen anyone transmit the energy and shape of music in this way, his hands beckoning, face open and glowing, sacred.

I quickly scanned the room and saw that everyone else was playing as if nothing were strange. Returning my eyes to him, I watched his arms flowing gracefully, baton drawing out the sounds of the musicians around me. The warmth of the symphonic band filled the room, shaping me. Later that week, without a second thought, I changed my major from music therapy to music education in order to accommodate a new vision of myself: I was going to become a conductor.

I began making the transition to conductor while at MSU, first learning the technique—the four-beat pattern, the three-beat pattern, the two-beat pattern, how to cue the trumpets, the percussion in an entrance, how to transmit the style of the piece through the tip of the baton. The technique of a conductor is important. The better the skills, the more effective the rehearsal, and the clearer the performance.

But technique is empty without the heart and humanity of the conductor. I have seen people on the podium with far less skill in the area of ictus and style who nevertheless transmitted the joy, the force, the tranquility of the music because they were able to embody the essence of the piece in their spirit. As an eighteen-year-old, I was not yet aware of myself as a spirit, but I knew that there was something beyond the physical aspect of conducting and performing that I was striving to reach, connect with, and possess.

With the backdrop of the changing colors on the MSU campus that autumn, I was initiated into a higher degree of music-making, the sky darkening a bit earlier each day, so that the sounds of rehearsal would follow us into the early evening twilight. I slipped and slid the twenty minutes back to my dorm along the icy paths of the Red Cedar River, my energy and spirit uplifted, the snap of the cold autumn air sharpening my awareness of new, light-filled spaces opening within me.

But as the presence of that light made apparent the gray-black days of winter, a scandal arose within the music department, and by the end of my freshman year, our conductor was forced to leave his position as Director of Bands at MSU. The surrounding circumstances were beyond my understanding at the time; allegations of sexual harassment and opposing opinions on all sides muddied the waters of reason like the brown, unfathomable current of the Red Cedar River. And like that swift-running river, we were carried into a future where all I truly understood was that I was heartbroken. My newfound experience of music as holy and sacred had ended in confusion and scandal, and the future of the MSU band program, and my place in it, were uncertain.

CHAPTER FOUR

SONG

U pon my return as a sophomore the following year, I auditioned yet again for placement in one of the three concert bands at MSU. We had a young, interim conductor for the quarter who had the responsibility of placing hundreds of us into the appropriate ensembles. I sailed through the audition, my tone clear and relaxed on an unaccompanied flute solo by Hindemith, despite the interim conductor's confusion as he shuffled through his stack of audition forms, his eyes flitting from one page to the other while I played.

The following day the results were posted outside of the rehearsal hall; I scanned the lists for my name and was devastated to learn that I had been placed in the lower Concert Band. Looking at the roster, none of the placements made any sense; musicians who regularly performed with the Lansing Symphony Orchestra had also been placed in the Concert Band. Turning on my heel, I marched into the interim director's office and pointedly asked him to explain the results. He scratched at his beard and spoke to the marble pencil holder on his desk, muttering, "Well, you know, sometimes the level of the band changes …" His non-beard-scratching hand waved above his head as his nonsensical reply dropped off into silence. I stared at him, shook my head, and turned on my heel one more time.

I choked back my tears of disappointment that evening as I considered my options for the fall's performance ensembles. The thought of not rehearsing with the Symphony Band was painful enough, but worse still was the idea of performing in the lowest ensemble. I simply could not stomach it, and my mind searched for a way out.

Scanning the ensemble options in the course catalog, my eyes lingered on "Women's Glee Club—non-audition." Glee Club? The name alone lifted my heart. Just saying the word "glee" elevated me to a gladder state of mind. Non-audition? No problem! I could sing and had learned how to sight-sing using solfege—do, re, mi—during my freshman music theory classes.

With one more march down the hallway to my advisor's office the next morning, I stood tall and declared that I would not participate in the Concert Band that season. I was going to sing in the Women's Glee Club! My ancient advisor cocked his head, eyebrows lifted above his glasses, and nodded as he signed the paperwork. He had fielded similar requests earlier that day as the School of Music strained under the weight of a leaderless department.

I floated out of his office, my heart smiling as headed to my first Glee Club rehearsal, clearing my throat.

"Raindrops are falling, forming clouds of water ..." The native melody arose within me as I stepped down the hallway toward the choral rehearsal room. I had learned it in fourth-grade music class and sung it to my sister late at night as we lied in the dark, her bed just a few feet from mine. My voice flowed into space, rising higher and higher with the minor, pentatonic melody. I was touched when my sister told me, "You have a good voice," for it is one of the earliest compliments regarding my musical abilities that I can remember.

The song stayed, fortifying me as I found myself in com-pletely new territory. I had never sung formally before, other than our weekly sight-singing classes as a part of freshman "ear training." But it was in this Women's Glee Club that I would dis-cover my joy in and ability to make music without the extension of an external instrument, only with the instrument that each one of us is born with—our voice.

The Women's Glee Club was a joyous musical experience unlike anything I had ever heard before. A contemporary setting of the Kyrie Eleison, or a playful melody with a text by Shake-speare, offered fresh flavors and textures as I explored my voice in the second alto section. I sang my parts as I returned to my dorm each evening, tones reverberating from deep within as I walked along the icy pathways next to the river. I pushed the traditional black garb that we instrumentalists wear to every concert to the back of my closet. Instead, we choristers adorned ourselves in colorful gowns of red, yellow, and blue in every style; we weren't trying to blend in. We were women in the height of our youth, with the big hairstyles and bright eye shadow of the mid-eighties; it was a theatrical experience, and my heart, healing from the trauma of the fall audition process, warmed to the new aesthetic.

When I had the opportunity to reaudition for the band program for the second and third quarters that year, the interim conductor, along with his flitting eyes and beard-scratching habit, had been let go, and the beloved professor of the concert and marching bands was at the helm for the remainder of the academic year. My audition went well, and I was placed back into the Symphony Band toward the top of the flute section. I felt vindicated, affirmed as a flute player, yet I continued to sing in the Technicolor Glee Club for another quarter, just for fun, cultivating my voice and learning about being in a vocal ensemble. I never imagined that decades later I would draw on this experience over and over again.

CHAPTER FIVE

KICK-STEP

As a freshman new to campus, I cried the first time I heard the MSU Spartan Marching Band, utterly disappointed that it was too late to join for the year. The sounds of this powerhouse group reverberated around campus from their practice spot on Landon Field, which was surrounded by tall pines, their shadows lengthening across the musicians during late afternoon rehearsals. I had to wait two years to make time for the band in my life. Since there were no flutes or clarinets in the band, I borrowed an old alto sax from the music department, taught myself the fundamentals, and auditioned for a slot in the fall of my junior year.

All marching band members reported to campus in early September, about two weeks before the academic year began, when the air had a hint of autumn though the days were still brutally hot. We learned to march in the early mornings, straining to lift our thighs parallel—or higher—to the grass on Landon Field. My borrowed saxophone was so old that some of the lower keys that are normally located on the right side of the sax were actually placed on the left side. When I kick-stepped— the running/march step that we did to enter the field—the keys would dig into my right ribs, causing painful bruising and, ultimately, after a few weeks, toughened skin, a badge, that would remain with me all season. We learned field drills for hours each day, alternated with indoor rehearsals—with over two hundred of us in the rehearsal room—where we learned fantastic and challenging arrangements to later be performed during our half-time shows. In a rush of adrenaline, I sat among close friends—Ann, Chrissy, and Ben—in the sax section, sunburnt and sweating during the long rehearsals, my ears filled with Peter Gunn and "Rhapsody in Blue," heart racing.

Lots of organizations have hazing rituals. The Spartan Marching Band, at least in the eighties, was no different. At first, the older members just made references to the "hayride" in a mocking tone. Throughout the two weeks of preseason rehearsals, which often lasted twelve to fourteen hours a day, the details of this ritual slowly emerged. In order to prepare for our initiation, we freshman—defined as anyone new to the organization—had to learn and memorize all of our music, which consisted of a number of pregame and half-time arrangements, as well as master the various marching steps we had drilled during those blistering afternoons. We often continued practicing until midnight. We knew we would be tested, so all of us newbies were nervous as the night of the "hayride" approached.

On the last day of our preseason band camp, we were told to report to a field behind some of the large dorms on the MSU campus late that night. I showed up along with the other fifty or so "freshman" with instrument in hand, apprehensive, hoping I would survive the experience. My friend Ann had withstood it two years earlier and would only share that she just wanted to "crawl under a rock and die" when it was over—no further details.

We were lined up in squads, drilled in marching techniques and the repertoire we learned, all the time being disparaged and insulted by the upperclassmen.

"Hey, you freshman!" they called out, circling our squad. "You sound awful!"

Understanding that this was a moment meant to tear down our egos, I set my jaw and paid attention to my breath; their jabs bypassed me and dissipated into the night air. The moment would pass, though I didn't know when. My fingers raced over the keys as I performed, on demand, the music I had memorized late at night in the basement practice rooms. Fight songs and jazz passed through my blistered lips, which scraped on the reed, my top teeth biting into the mouthpiece. My squad leader shouted out drill commands—left face, right face, pinwheel! I was a robot, ignoring the fact that we had already been on the field for many hours earlier that day.

Time passed, elastic, surreal. We stood at attention, numb, while the upperclassmen huddled for a moment. When they broke their huddle, it was with renewed vitriol, barking orders for us to join our squads together into one band.

"Move your butts, freshmen! Let's see what you can really do!"

Fifty of us initiates, now worn down both physically and mentally, began marching through campus. There is a particular drum cadence called "The Series" that is used whenever the MSU marching band is on parade. The cadence is technically challenging for the percussionists, and the rest of us instrumentalists have a complicated series of calls and moves that we make as it progresses; each night throughout the preseason, often until midnight, the freshman worked on learning all the parts of this sequence. Our horns flashed under the lights, gripped tightly by our sweaty hands, as the drums thrummed in our chests.

As we marched through campus that night—the night of the "hayride"—we executed the moves, at first accompanied by the jeering of the upperclassmen. Amidst the insults and taunts, our muscles cramping, our eyes tearing with effort, lungs gasping for air, something was happening. We strained together, bonded, and began drawing strength from each other, from the drum cadence, from our whoops and calls synchronized to the movement of "The Series." In between verses of the fight song, there were smiles among the ranks, ours shoulders close together as our feet struck the pavement. We had no idea what time it was, or when we had last eaten, or how long this "hayride" would go on for, but we knew that we were making it through together, and that was all that mattered.

We proceeded through campus, passing dormitories with blackened windows where everyone else was sleeping. Coming closer and closer to the bridge that crossed the Red Cedar River, we were soothed by the suddenly cooler air, and we realized that there were no longer 150 or so upperclassmen running alongside us, yelling and criticizing, as they had been all evening. They had already crossed the bridge, some 200 yards in front of us, no longer taunting but cheering us on, calling out encouragement.

"Come on, you can do it! You're great; we love you—yeahhh-hhhh!" rang out in waves of strength that I could feel in my chest.

The moment had come for us to be built up, united with the entire band, initiated. The drum cadence grew louder, our legs raised higher, our voices calling out "The Series" with conviction and joy, tears streaming down our faces as we approached the bridge. I was carried across on a current of energy and sound, my heart bursting with relief and a visceral sense of union with my squad members and the upperclassmen who were congratulating and hugging us, welcoming us as full members of the MSU Spartan Marching Band.

The "hayride" ended at 4 a.m. on a quiet campus. The river had borne witness to our courage and union, the vibrations recorded in its depths.

Gathered in a tight group, arms encircling each other, we sang "Shadows," the alma mater song, in four-part harmony.

Years later, when I returned to participate in the alumni marching band, we marched "The Series" again, but this time our group, ranging in age from twenty-three to seventy-plus, marched to a slower tempo that allowed us to raise our aging knees more comfortably and breathe a little easier as we marched through the streets of the MSU campus. We smiled as we passed the onlookers lining the streets of campus on that September day, for we weren't in a rush and had nothing to prove. After the festivities of the game, we returned once again to Landon Field. We alumni, survivors of "hayrides" past, had earned the privilege of singing in four-part harmony our beloved alma mater, and as only alumni were allowed, we sang the second and final verse.

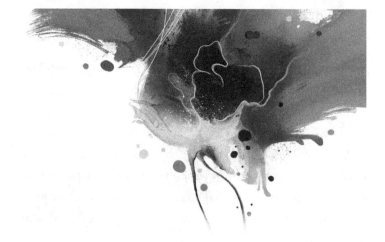

CHAPTER SIX

VASSAR

I n 1986, I successfully completed my degree in music education at MSU and went on to snag my first teaching position as an assistant band director in the small, rural town of
Vassar in the "thumb" of Michigan. My first "real" job consisted
of a daily schedule teaching fifth- and sixth-grade beginning
band, eighth-grade band, high school symphonic band, and color
guard for the marching band. My life moved to a new rhythm
in this small town with one supermarket, one gas station, and
one good restaurant, which unfortunately was destroyed only
weeks after I moved there. Rains so fierce and abundant caused
the Cass River to overflow, and the National Guard had to be

brought in. I witnessed all of this safely from the second-floor studio apartment I rented for only 165 dollars per month.

I cut my teeth as a young conductor with fabulous kids who gave me the chance to rehearse my beloved "First Suite" in E-flat by Gustav Holst. Our early morning rehearsals were filled with drilling the complicated notes. My students worked diligently, not because they appreciated or understood the piece necessarily, but because they were simply well-behaved kids doing as they were told.

I divided up parts, alternating measures of sixteenth notes between the girls in the clarinet section—Tanya, Marty, and Laura—so they would not have to play continuous, rapid runs (which they did not have the technique for anyway), and worked my trumpet players' ranges higher and higher so they could approach the final notes of the first movement.

When I told the director of the program, Bob, that my second-string high school band would perform this piece at the district competition, his eyes widened in disbelief as he exclaimed, "You're going to get slaughtered!" With my twenty-two-year-old arrogance, I proceeded as planned, patiently working my students throughout the winter while the snow piled up outside.

There is a moment during the rehearsal process when musicians reach a level of comfort and confidence with the technical aspects of a piece and can finally open up their hearts and allow their feelings and expression to animate and enliven the music. This happens even with the youngest musicians, beginning band students who are barely out of the honking and squeaking phase, all the way up to professionals. At this moment, the piece and all of its technical components has a force of its own, capable of transmitting energy back to the musician and out to the audience. There is a synergy, an open channel between the musician and the rest of the universe, the music a carrier of profound depths of feeling and wisdom.

In our rehearsal room, the symphonic band members were awakening to the magical synergy of the Holst suite. They arrived each day at 8 a.m.—dressed warmly in flannel shirts and boots, having already tended to the cows on their family farms—and began to invest themselves and their feelings as they played during those cold, gray February mornings.

We earned top scores a month later at the competition, due in equal parts to my bullheadedness and the growing talent of those sweet kids. As we loaded up the yellow school buses afterward, instruments stored in the dusty compartments underneath, Bob shook his head graciously and said, "I heard those kids playing notes that they've never played before."

CHAPTER SEVEN

CINCINNATI

I n that same year, at barely twenty-three years old, I married my college sweetheart. We arranged and decorated our new apartment with the scads of engagement and wedding gifts we received—food processors, silver platters and tea sets, crystal candle sticks—playing house and naively enjoying the routine of our newly married life. I drove twenty-six miles to school in the dark, winter mornings beneath gray, leaden skies after scraping eight inches of newly fallen snow and ice off my windshield.

After two years of early mornings, six classes per day, and school lunches, I was itching for a new setting, a return to academia. The man who served as Director of Bands during my last two years at MSU, Eugene Corporon, had accepted a new position at the College-Conservatory of Music at the University of Cincinnati. As Director of Wind Studies, he had the authority to offer me a full scholarship and a teaching assistantship in the music education department. So we moved from the biting cold of Michigan winters to the sweltering humidity along the Ohio River.

Thomas Jefferson stated, "The Ohio is the most beautiful river on earth. Its current gentle, waters clear, and bosom smooth and unbroken by rocks and rapids, a single instance only excepted." It was along this river that I left the naiveté of my first marriage, though the process was not gentle, nor unbroken by rocks and rapids. Perhaps I was the "single instance only excepted." My first husband, Eric, was a good man—how could we have possibly known what we wanted out of life at such a young age?

I found myself more often drawn to the spiritual realm, reading the mystical stories of Carlos Castaneda and his shaman teacher, Don Juan, late into the night. These books were introduced to me years earlier at MSU by Eugene through the music of Michael Colgrass's "Winds of the Nagual," which we had played in the Wind Symphony. I played the alto flute solo in the third movement, entitled "Carlos Stares at the River and Becomes a Bubble," and was hooked.

At the new-age bookstore down the block, I purchased a copy of Shakti Gawain's *Living in the Light* and something moved deep within me—a longing to meditate, to perceive something beyond the black-and-white tile of our "yuppie" railroad apartment and small, but growing, investment portfolio.

A tug-of-war between the material and the spiritual, a chasm widened between us, with no bridge to the other side.

As our second summer in Cincinnati drew to a close, I rented an apartment in a questionable neighborhood on the other side of campus; it was a five-floor walk-up, and I stubbornly dragged my possessions up to the fifth floor, including an oak dining table that I had won in a bitter fight with Eric. Thus began our trial separation, which deep in my heart I knew wasn't actually a trial. The moment I moved into my uninsulated apartment, sweltering in the August heat and freezing in the winters to come, I knew I would never go back.

My life took on an air of simplicity. As a graduate student, I earned a 600-dollar stipend each month. My rent was only 230 dollars per month, and I had a car that was paid for. My daily lunch was a ninety-six-cent bean burrito from Taco Bell. I was content to wear the same ripped jeans and black tunic every day, and I shaved my head in a buzz cut, hoping I could get away with it like Sinéad O'Connor. Everything in my life was stripped down to essentials so that I could focus inward on the murky waters of my emotions.

During the day, I taught my classes, attended others, and rehearsed with the Wind Symphony under Eugene's baton. But at night, I would play Tracy Chapman's "Crossroads" CD or Mickey Hart's "Planet Drum" on my Sony boom box and dance, unrestrained, amidst the cheap furniture and houseplants in my new apartment. I grew basil on the fire escape that I would later sprinkle on my pasta.

I was grateful to be alone as I began to process what I had been through in my marriage. I allowed myself to feel raw anger, grief, and uncertainty as I whirled, cried, and stomped on the hardwood floors; it never occurred to me to wonder what the downstairs neighbors might have heard or thought.

Oh, the peace I experienced every time I honored whatever it was that I was feeling; the solitude was healing, and I grew firm in the knowledge that I was never going back to my marriage with Eric. I had no idea what I was headed toward, but I trusted that it would inherently be good—and completely of my own design.

We filed for divorce that autumn, arguing over the division of money and possessions. All I really wanted was to move forward and, feeling guilty about the way I had mishandled our relationship in previous months, I signed the papers and prayed that the ninety days until our divorce was final would pass quickly and painlessly. I pressed on every day, drained, as winter approached.

Winters in Cincinnati can be bitterly cold and damp, and that winter was no exception, especially in my uninsulated walk-up. I put plastic over the windows, but my apartment faced northwest, so the winds penetrated through the walls anyway and settled on the scratched, wooden floors. The ceilings were high; any warmth that managed to radiate from the steam heaters was swept upward without so much as a brief pause to warm the futon on which I slept.

Our divorce was finalized in January. I showed up at the courthouse wearing my standard uniform of black boots, a bomber jacket, and my shaved head. At twenty-five, I lacked the maturity to dress more formally. I showed up alone, while Eric had his mother with him—why, I do not know, but I judged him for it anyway, as had become my habit. The proceedings were brief and unremarkable, the judge rubber-stamping a line of former couples' "uncontested" divorces with no expression on his face, legally establishing a new chapter for everyone who passed in front of him.

Afterward, in the cavernous lobby, Eric wished me well, his mother respectfully waiting some fifteen feet away. I couldn't manage anything other than a mumbled "goodbye," and escaping out of the courthouse onto the windy street, I entered a new moment, sleet stinging my face, boots hollowly striking the ground.

But out of that emotional darkness and icy Cincinnati winter, a musical flower bloomed. I truly do not know how it came to me, but I was offered an honor band conducting position in Dayton, OH—about one hour north of Cincinnati—every Saturday morning for a two-month period. Perhaps the musings of a guest professor years earlier at MSU were true—that I had radiated a light into the universe and attracted the perfect job. I hadn't applied for the position, but apparently someone had spoken to someone else, and I found myself in front of a forty-piece band of high school musicians—some of them quite good—who had auditioned to earn a place in the ensemble. I set myself to the program in my usual ambitious way, dressed in my black suit and heels, and drove north every Saturday throughout that winter. The kids were wonderful—trusting and obedient. They came well-prepared to every rehearsal as I pushed them through the challenging set of pieces I had chosen.

One of those pieces was "Elegy for a Young American" by American composer Ronald LoPresti, which was written in honor of John F. Kennedy only a few years after he was assassinated. It is a heavy piece; there is no sugarcoating in the dissonant harmonies played by the clarinets in the opening theme. In heartrending anguish, the music moves at a stately tempo, instrument sections joining one by one, octave upon octave in searing melodies that are not designed to coddle or protect us from the harshness of this story. Once the music sinks its hooks into your heart, there is no respite as it builds toward its shocking and devastating climax, the pounding of the timpani representing the gunshot that ended this young American's life and the optimism that he instilled in the U.S. until that moment. The closing chord offers only a slight lightening of the heart, a tentative peace and stillness where we can collect ourselves, shaken, and begin to conceive how to move forward.

My honor band students and I worked our way through the complexities of this piece every Saturday morning. They didn't complain that it wasn't "fun" or lighthearted, nor did they ask that we play familiar pop music instead. They embraced it wholly, connecting with the shared human experience of loss and suffering. We were all so young; my guess is that most of us in that rehearsal room had never experienced tragedy firsthand, but when we performed "Elegy" early that spring for an auditorium full of parents, siblings, and band directors, the audience sat in stunned silence for a few seconds after the final chord, finding themselves, I imagine, in new territory, uprooted, unsure how to move forward.

Even today, five decades after "Elegy" was composed, you can read the remarks of high school and college band students online describing how they are unable to get through the piece without crying. This speaks to the sheer power music has to connect us through a shared experience. Whether or not I or my honor band students had experienced loss, through the performance of one piece of music, we were connected vibrationally. Without sharing words or stories, we could feel the same depth of tragedy and frailty of life in each of our hearts.

We said our farewells in the auditorium lobby after our performance, sharing shy embraces and well wishes for the future. I walked out to the parking lot, high heels clicking on the cold concrete. I had made it through another Cincinnati winter; the days were growing longer and the trees hinted faintly with green buds that would arrive in the next few weeks. I drove the hour back to my neighborhood and rewarded myself with a five-dollar enchilada from the Mexican restaurant around the corner and a new bar of sandalwood soap—at one dollar and eighty-nine cents, the soap was a cheap splurge. Parking my car blocks away from my apartment, I cradled a can of mace in my hand, always on the lookout for a potential threat in the "sketchy" neighborhood where I lived, the vibrations of "Elegy" still circulating within me.

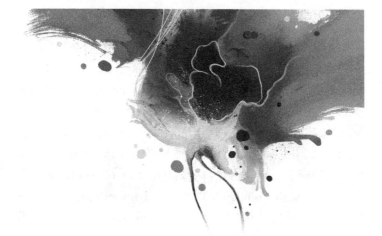

CHAPTER EIGHT

WESTWARD FLIGHT

Two years later, I was driving a 2,400 mile stretch from Cincinnati to Seattle, WA. Master of Music degree in hand, I had gotten a job as Director of Bands at Evergreen Junior High School in Redmond, the east suburbs of Seattle, only a few miles away from a man, Tristan, I had been in a relationship with for the past few months.

My friend Kate agreed to come along for the trip to Seattle, and we cruised through the rural towns of Indiana and Illinois in my red Honda Civic, eating junk food and gabbing the whole way. Those first couple of states still felt like my Midwestern home, with spacious, neat farmlands and the occasional rolling hill.

But as we travelled toward South Dakota and eventually on Interstate 90, which would bring us the remaining 1,500-plus miles to Seattle, the landscape changed distinctly, opening into broad and looming vistas as we entered what are known as the "Badlands" just south of the highway. The name alone doesn't bring about a warm, fuzzy feeling, nor does the ocean of rock formations with foundations formed eighty million years ago from a great inland sea. The Lakota people were the first to call the area by this particular name because of its extreme temperatures and lack of water and vegetation.

On the outskirts of the national park, we noticed a small, hand-painted sign advertising helicopter tours of the park. Kate and I glanced at each other, and without saying a word, I pulled off the road into a cloud of dust. We hopped out of the car and practically ran toward a stubbled, older man with a crew cut who gamely limped toward us.

"Can we get a ride today?" we asked him, noticing his backward glance toward a sky growing thick with nimbus clouds.

"Well, I suppose so, as long as we make it a quick one," he replied, scratching the back of his neck.

A range of helicopter ride options were scrawled on the chipped, wooden sign. Since we didn't have much money, we opted for the "micro-hop," a five-minute trip into just the beginning of the Badlands. I figured I had just enough courage to handle five minutes in a helicopter, so we informed the man of our choice and climbed aboard.

One striking feature about helicopters is that they do not have doors. This might seem obvious, and unproblematic, if you are viewing them from the security of the ground, but once you are inside of one, climbing quickly and abruptly toward steep canyon rock, it can be quite terrifying. Add to this scenario a loose-fitting, frayed seatbelt that had clearly seen better days and a threatening sky with winds that blew straight through the helicopter. The complete picture includes me gripping the loose seatbelt, screaming, inwardly praying to God that I would not fall out and die this way.

My friend Kate, however—always the adventurer—leaned way out the door, arms flung out in the wind, as our pilot whisked us into the canyon at a slight tilt, hugging the landscape as the blades roared above us. Seeing Kate opening herself to the moment with the glee of a child, I realized that I, too, could do this, for if I were going to die this way, I might as well whoop it up while I still could. So, I whooped aloud and opened my eyes to the remarkable landscape through which we sped, laughing hysterically—though I never did let go of the frayed seatbelt.

Within moments we found ourselves back on the ground, exiting the craft with shaky legs and tears rolling down our faces. With one quick look at each other, Kate and I exclaimed in a flash, "Let's do it again!" Our captain chuckled heartily as we hopped aboard, strapping ourselves in for one more "micro-hop." But he so enjoyed our enthusiasm that he gave us a much longer tour the second time. Hugging the canyon walls, he dipped and ducked the helicopter into large, shadowed caves, which could not ever be seen on foot. My stomach plummeted with each upward thrust. The wind whipped our hair in our faces; the scent of rain was forced up our nostrils and we had to breathe through our mouths as we continued celebrating our surprise at each twist and turn.

Finally, out of breath and exhilarated, we returned to the landing pad as the summer storm opened up and began pelting our faces and bare arms. We hugged and thanked our pilot, who was shaking his head in wonderment at our joy. With the broad vistas of the Badlands implanted in our hearts, we folded ourselves back into my little Honda Civic and headed west.

Crossing the continental divide in Montana, I felt dwarfed by the Rocky Mountains—in a good way. For the first time in my life, I was realizing the bigness of Nature and how small I was in comparison. Until that moment I had lived largely surrounded by pavement and manmade structures, sheltered from the reality of earth's nature, its beauty and its power. We camped in Montana for one night in order to save some money on hotels, and the scent of the rising sun on the damp pines nearly knocked me over when I exited the tent.

Here was something completely new to me, at the age of twenty-seven. Nature itself was becoming a character in my life, and a prominent one at that. I was just starting to perceive the changes that might happen within me, recalling the times years earlier when I devoured books by Carlos Castaneda while huddled in my comfortable Michigan apartment, yearning for some kind of experience that I could not put into words. As we crossed Montana and the panhandle of Idaho, into Washington's dry and dusty eastern plains across the Cascades to the verdant, dense air of western Washington, this awareness persisted. I had crossed into new territory—not only the frontier of our country but a foreign border within my consciousness.

CHAPTER NINE

SEATTLE RAINS

arly each morning, beginning at 7 a.m., my band room would fill with new faces for me to learn—junior high kids from the wealthy east-side suburbs of Seattle. Collars turned up on their Izod polo shirts, their loafers skimmed across the waxed floor, expensive instruments making the daily trip home and back—these kids actually practiced! They were confident, well-bred, and made easy work of Vaclav Nelhybel's "Festivo" and Frank Erickson's "Air for Band." They ate up the rhythm exercises I wrote daily on the white board and high-fived me on their way out of class each day, their backpacks loaded with algebra and earth science texts.

Having settled into a routine of teaching and performing in the Seattle area, I again began to turn inward, examining the happenings in my life as reflections of who I was as an evolving spirit, searching for my tribe—and with it, a more specific spiritual path. My seeking brought me to a new-age Jewish reformed temple one week, complete with folk guitar and vocals, and to a meditation class on the far side of Lake Washington another week, where the meditation leader, wide-eyed and fanatical, spoke for thirty minutes against the practice of routine circumcision here in the United States. I made the mistake of bringing my visiting mother to this particular class. God only knows what she thought of my spiritual exploration at that point, but she graciously sat through the hour-long meditation and ensuing lecture on "genital mutilation" as only a loving mother can.

And, as only a mother could know her daughter, she saw that despite my content routine, I was deeply unhappy in my relationship with Tristan. I walked on eggshells around him, often feeling misunderstood. An evening together could easily turn from easy dinner banter to a full-blown argument about what seemed to be an insignificant fact or perception. I found myself making excuses for the way he was, building up his professional talent and intellect unnecessarily. And as I explored my spirituality more, his tone became increasingly sardonic, eyes rolled upward as he turned away from the conversation with a dismissive shrug.

It's possible that I am exaggerating his response to my spiritual growth; maybe I was simply projecting some unknown critical and judgmental voice within me, but this is what I remember through my filtered perception. Hence, I was unfulfilled in this dramatic relationship, which was as dark and gloomy as the winter sky in Seattle. Still on her week-long visit with me, my mother simply said, "You know, Rhonda, you can be happy."

These seven words managed to penetrate my despair like a sun beam through the low ceiling of clouds in the Pacific Northwest—because they were spoken with the force of a mother's love. I smiled weakly in response, and though it would still take a couple of months for me to act on them, those words of counsel had landed in my young, incubating spirit and taken root. Like tender blades of grass breaking through the concrete sidewalk and reaching for the sun, my mother's words began to crack the foundation of my illusion that I simply did not deserve any more happiness than I currently had. And as winter gave way to the warmth of spring, my residual guilt regarding my failed first marriage washed away.

It was on a rain-soaked evening in the parking lot of Tristan's apartment building, upon returning from dinner, that we began to fight about God knows what. We stood out there, bickering underneath the streetlight as it filtered through the drizzle. It was just enough illumination for me to see the scowl on his face—and the weariness in my soul.

In that moment of clarity, I said, "Hey, look what we're doing. We're fighting again. I don't want to do this anymore. I'm getting off the roller coaster."

I wasn't angry. On the contrary, I felt love and compassion for myself and for him. Neither one of us deserved this kind of circus and drama in our lives. His head snapped back and he asked, "What do you mean?"

"Tristan, we've been doing this for some time now. Back and forth, like we're riding a roller coaster. I'm getting off now," I exclaimed, the realization spreading across my face as I backed away from him, heading toward my car. I crossed the parking lot erect, victorious, the scent of pine and rain watering my spirit.

CHAPTER TEN

SWEAT

I haven't sung in nine years, not since my glorious Glee Club days at MSU. Only two months after the breakup with Tristan, I am about to participate in my first sweat lodge. I learned about it from a flyer posted in the Stone House Bookstore, where I've become a regular. I attended classes there with names like "Preparing for the Coming Earth Changes" and "Healing with Crystals." On a Saturday morning, I drive toward the Cascade Mountains on I-90, the directions to the sweat lodge leader's house written on the back of the flyer, my stomach unsettled with anticipation and excitement.

The sweat lodge is a low, rounded structure made of bent willow branches, thickly covered with blankets so that no light can penetrate once the flap door is closed. It is a representation of the womb of the Earth, a place where we can purify ourselves—physically and spiritually—through the placement of hot stones and water that create an intense steam in the center of the lodge. We will enter the lodge through a low door, crawling like children, humble—a good quality to have on any spiritual path.

Before we enter the lodge, John, the sixty-something-year-old man who will lead us in the ritual, appraises each one of us, all women, observing our nervous laughter and says, "Well, I guess we'll go easy on you all, since this is your first time."

None of us has any bravado at this point, so we smile weakly, gratefully at this man's wisdom and prudence. We follow him to the backyard, stubbing our bare toes on the flagstone path. There is a smoky fire outside the sweat lodge, attended by a bearded, younger man, where the large, river stones have already been heating for some hours. Feeling the intense heat of the fire, I wonder how I will fare once inside the lodge. As we line up to enter, our leader waves a combination of burning cedar and sage up and down the length of our bodies, back and front, even under our feet; its smoke begins the process of purification. On our knees we crawl headfirst into the darkness, into another world, "Aho Mitakuye Oyasin" on our lips, the Lakota saying for "All Our Relations."

We feel our way around the perimeter of the sweat lodge, forming a circle around the pit in the center where the stones will eventually be placed. Settling into a cross-legged position, I inhale deeply, breathing the lingering scent of cedar and sage, and await our leader's instructions. He explains that we will pass through four rounds of prayers accompanied by increasing numbers of heated stones and water. He encourages us to open ourselves up, to be humble, to call out our prayers to Great Spirit. And without any further directions, he calls to his fire tender to send in seven stones.

The rocks come in on a long shovel, glowing with "eyes" that see right through me. They are placed in the center pit, only about a foot or so from our bare shins.

"Close the flap!" John commands with a flourish, and immediately we are in complete darkness, the womb of the Earth, the bottom of our spirits. One might think that in the dark, we can hide. But without my exterior—my face, my clothing, my profession, my personality—visible, I feel naked before God. There is no pretense, no facade, no rescue from what lies ahead.

We are told that the first round is dedicated to the East direction, the place of all beginnings, where the sun rises, where clarity and illumination can enter so that we may have an eagle's perspective on what we need to purify within ourselves and our lives. After pouring several ladles of water on the hot stones, releasing a torrent of searing steam into our faces, John directs us to start praying, out loud, for what we need to see. Already shocked by the heat, my first prayer is that I can make it through this.

Tentatively, self-consciously, each one of us begins. I wonder, "What if someone hears what I am asking for?" But I feel a force within me growing, a lion's courage to embrace this opportunity, and I hear my voice rising along with the other women's pleas, calling on Great Spirit to help me—to help us—see what has been hidden.

We continue, for how long I do not know, the hot steam opening our lungs, scorching our faces (Did I really wear mascara today?), removing any vestiges of arrogance. I sweat through my white tank top immediately, and feeling faint, wonder how I will survive three more rounds of this.

When I believe that I cannot stand another second of the intense heat, John ceremoniously calls out, "Open the flap!" to which the fire tender immediately responds. The heat and steam rush out the door, and we seven women collapse on the ground, lying sideways on each other, gulping in the cool air with relief.

After a few moments of quiet and introspection, our leader, who has been seated near the door the entire time, calls out, "Bring in five more stones!" Five more? I can only imagine the exponential increase in heat that five more stones will bring. I right myself, take a deep breath, and close my eyes as the flap is closed once again and we are back in the darkness, the ladles of water hissing at us.

In this second round, the lessons of the South direction are presented to us—teachings of childlike trust and humility and the admonition of not taking ourselves too seriously, which is frankly a lifelong curriculum for me. My mascara, which at this point is dripping down my face and stinging my eyes, makes it hard for me to take myself seriously, so I settle into the out-loud prayers once again, asking to be cleaned of my arrogance and all the things I think I know about myself and life. I pray to be more trusting, less fearful and controlling. The heat is unbearable, and I find myself lying down halfway through the round with my nose perched in the crack between the blanketed wall and the earth, praying for a drop of cool air.

And thus, I am humbled like a child, needy and weak. I lie here for a long time, the prayers of the women encircling me in a web of emotion. When the flap is finally raised, I realize that I am not the only one lying facedown in the mud. Most of us have succumbed, which I realize is part of the plan. Purification of the spirit is not a comfortable task. We don't come to it dressed in high heels, wearing mascara. We come on our knees, and if we are not on our knees at first, then, rest assured, we will be on our knees eventually, realizing that we don't know anything at all.

Slowly we all sit up, sagging with exhaustion, smiling weakly at each other, and nodding our encouragement, "We're doing this we've got this." We pass around a tin cup of water, sharing it from one mouth to the other—no one cares about germs at this point. I barely know these women's names, but they have become my sisters with each drop of sweat, with each tear, with each prayer. Our naked eyes gleam at each other, reflecting the diminishing light outside. I wonder what time it is, realizing that the afternoon is turning into early evening. I don't know if we have been in the lodge for twenty minutes or two hours at this point, and comically the lyrics of Chicago's song rise within me as I realize I don't know what time it is, nor do I care.

With a thundering voice that wakes me out of my reverie, John calls, "Send in six more stones!" and one by one, they appear on the long shovel, creating a mound in the pit that illuminates the faces of everyone in the circle.

"Close the flap!" he calls again. "This is the direction of the West, the place of the setting sun and all tomorrows. This is where we face our fears and gather our courage to know our truth and to move toward what we want in our lives. This is the place of Bear medicine."

John tosses more water on the hot stones. Wave after wave of steam crests over our heads, and once again we begin praying out loud for courage, for truth to come to us. After some moments, arising clearly from the blur of prayers, John's voice sings out an unfamiliar song.

> "Yanni o we ah ho way nay. Yanni o we ah ho way nay.
> Oh we ah ho way nay, hay nay. Yanni o we ah ho way nay."

Over and over again, he repeats this chant among our prayers, until one by one, we join in, feeling the courage of Bear, the West, our dreams. As our voices grow stronger, I feel my own from deep in my chest fill the sweat lodge and rise up to God—not in an attempt to cover anyone else's voice, but in a celebration of our Creator, raw and wild.

I sing—SING—for the first time in nine years, and my life is in Technicolor once again. The struggles of my first marriage, graduate school, the roller coaster relationship with Tristan and its ending are lifted from me on a voice that I do not recognize yet as my own. It is strong, resonant and clear, and it fills the sweat lodge, beating against the layers of blankets, the limitations within myself, persistently and valiantly.

I cry, and even though the heat is more intense than it was in the first two rounds, I withstand it, filled with a new light and strength.

We finish the third round as the chant fades and, taking only a brief pause once the door is opened, four final stones are passed in and the flap is quickly closed. We have arrived at the fourth round, the place of the North direction from which comes wisdom and gratitude. Calling out our prayers of thanks, a victorious energy circulates throughout the sweat lodge. And once again, amidst the prayers, John initiates a song.

> "The river she keeps flowing, flowing and growing,
> The river she keeps flowing, down to the sea.
> Mother, carry me, your child I will always be.
> Mother, carry me, down to the sea."

We learn the chant quickly, joyfully, singing our thanks to the waters. The heat and steam from the twenty-two stones feels like a cleansing bath, gentle, the touch of a mother. We smile at each other across the glow emanating from the pit, holding each other's sweaty hands, our faces glistening.

When the flap is opened for the final time, we crawl out as we came in, on our hands and knees, thanking the Earth for supporting us through the ritual. We stand up for the first time in three hours around the fire, rewarming ourselves, sticky with sweat, in the cool evening air. It is a rare clear night in the Pacific Northwest, so the stars twinkle above us as we settle into an appreciative and solemn silence. Sometime later, we walk back to the house to enjoy a potluck meal, the vibrations of the sweat lodge chants still reverberating within us, spiritually reborn.

On that day, a new type of music entered my life: the songs of the sweat lodge. My voice claimed them, and they became as much a part of my musical foundation as the works of Holst, Grainger, and Vaughn Williams. I hummed them to myself as I walked through the lunch line at Evergreen Junior High School, or as my students entered the band room. I sang them at my altar to initiate or end a time of meditation. Years later, I would sing them to my little daughter as we watched the setting sun in the west, her voice rising up, true and clear, to meet mine.

CHAPTER ELEVEN

SPIRIT

The Evergreen Point Floating Bridge is one of the largest floating pontoon bridges in the world, the floating portion sitting at 2,350 meters long. Having crossed the bridge many times on Washington State Route 520, which connects the east suburbs of Seattle where I reside to the downtown area, I felt like I was familiar with every crack in the pavement, every splash of water from Lake Washington below. More often than not, I was stuck in rush-hour traffic on my way to an evening event downtown.

It has been almost three years since I crossed the country from Cincinnati, through the Badlands of South Dakota and over the Cascade Mountains in central Washington. On this particular March evening in 1994, I am on my way to perform with the Washington Wind Symphony, a professional concert band; I play in the flute section. We rehearse on Monday evenings in my school's band room—teachers, attorneys, accountants, computer programmers—hashing out melodies by Grainger and transcriptions of Tchaikovsky and Shostakovich. My inner high-school nerd is grateful to have been invited to play upon my arrival in Washington; perhaps they let me in because they were, after all, rehearsing in my band room, with its fine percussion equipment and brand-new music stands (Evergreen Junior High is in the heart of Microsoft-land, so its music department was fully funded). Nonetheless, I have earned my keep in the organization and I revel in the sounds that we make, so much more refined than those of the junior high kids—though they are fabulous—with whom I spend my days.

On this March evening, I leave my home in Redmond with plenty of time to spare, but after fifteen minutes of sitting in traffic on the bridge, I become impatient and annoyed. We are at a dead stop, likely due to an accident miles ahead, so I daydream about a meeting I attended a few weeks earlier with some fellow teachers from Evergreen Junior High.

The four of us met in my apartment to brainstorm the possibility of opening a charter school. Disillusioned by the ringing bells, poor administrators, and bureaucracy of working in a large district, we commiserated in between bites of Stella D'oro cookies and sips of herbal tea. We fantasized about a "perfect" school, one where students and teachers would start each day with yoga and meditation. The arts would take a front-row seat rather than being relegated to thirty minutes at the end of the school day, just as our kids were rushing off to catch the bus to an afternoon track meet. We weren't the only teachers who dreamed of such an idyllic situation, but we were enthusiastic about the possibility and equally excited to realize that others shared our vision.

We said our goodbyes after a couple of hours of dreaming and furious note-taking, my colleagues descending the stairs into the steady drizzle that soaked the surrounding Douglas firs and oak trees. The evening scent awakened a memory of a conversation three years earlier regarding my future in education. The conversation had been recorded, so after shutting the front door, I raced to my file cabinet to locate the cassette tape. After digging through various documents and finding nothing but paper cuts, I gave up. Somewhere between Cincinnati and Redmond, the cassette had disappeared.

Back in my car on the floating bridge, with the traffic remaining at a standstill, I root around in my glove box, searching for the tape just one more time. Behind my registration documents, wedged tight in the corner, my fingers finally find the cracked, plastic cassette case and pry it loose. "Marguerite, June, 1991" is handwritten on the label. It is a ninety-minute "channeling" session I attended three years earlier in Cincinnati, just before my move to Seattle.

In 1991 I didn't even know what a "channel" was, but my friend Sherri told me how this woman—Marguerite—had gone into a trance and known things about Sherri that no one else could have known, giving her much-needed perspective on where she was in her life and what she ought to be doing. After hearing Sherri's story, my only response was, "Why not?"

I called Marguerite's number and booked a session with her for the following week.

Her house was located in an older neighborhood of Cincinnati, on a cul-de-sac surrounded by oaks and hickories. She greeted me at the door, an indistinguishably multi-racial woman dressed in coveralls and sporting a long black braid. Marguerite's home was comfortably messy with books and craft projects covering most of the surfaces, her husband and bright-eyed daughter in the background doing chores and homework, conversing easily.

It couldn't have been a more normal-looking family or home, as Marguerite seated me at the kitchen table, clearing some plates out of the way. She knew I was there for a reading, so she didn't waste any time exchanging much in the way of pleasantries. We were two strangers who knew only each other's names. She set a tape recorder on the table, inserted a blank cassette, and pressed the "record" button.

"Rhonda, I'm going to close my eyes and connect with Spirit now—just give me a moment. After the reading, I will come back, but I won't remember anything that happened during our time together."

What else could I say but, "Okay." I was in her hands from that point forward, so I opened myself to receiving what was to come.

Marguerite closed her eyes, took a few breaths, and stilled herself. After a moment, eyes still closed, an amused expression crossed her face as she shook her head and chuckled good-naturedly. When she finally opened her eyes, she was clearly "someone else." Her eyes showed a masculine energy, and when she spoke, her voice was a completely different tone, lower and more authoritative than when she greeted me at the door.

Still smiling, she said, "I don't know why I am seeing this, but I see you at the front of a marching band, conducting with one of those big sticks and leading the way."

My eyebrows rose at her vision; I was flabbergasted. There was no way that Marguerite could have known about my background as a conductor or of my experience in marching bands. When I called to make the appointment, I shared no details about my life. Marguerite, eyes closed once again, continued to enjoy this vision of me, shaking her head and smiling, wondering why I was at the head of the marching band.

"Umm, I guess I should tell you a little about myself," I said, and I proceeded to give her a brief statement about my professional life and education. She nodded and laughed, the vision which came from "Spirit" as she called it, finally making sense.

"Well, what is it that you want to know today?" the channel asked, settling into her chair with a different posture than in her pretrance state, shoulders squared back and chin lifted.

"Well, um, I'm looking for a teaching position in the Seattle area. I have a boyfriend there, but I'm wondering if I'm headed in the right direction."

Her face darkened for a moment, brow furrowed as she shook her head and exclaimed, "Oh, no, no, no—your kindred spirit are in the snowcapped mountains of Colorado."

She said these words definitively, and as they made their way across the crumb-covered Formica kitchen table and pierced my heart, I knew them to be true. It didn't matter that I had never been to Colorado before. I didn't even know exactly where it was on the map. I had some childhood friends who had moved to Montrose, Colorado about ten years earlier. My teenage impression was that Montrose was essentially a "Podunk" town (This, of course, was from the perspective of someone who had grown up only fourteen miles from Manhattan, the cultural epicenter just a bus trip away). I remember my friends telling me that they had to drive about sixty miles to see a rock concert in Grand Junction. Sixty miles? That was like driving to another state!

But all of these thoughts were as insignificant as the crumbs on the table, for I knew that I was in the presence of the wisdom of God in that moment.

Up until that point in my life, I had willingly gone along with what I "should" do—what made sense, what was reasonable, and what stemmed from my own ideas about how the world works. Being at the receiving end of Marguerite's words—or whoever was speaking through her—and seeing so clearly "the snowcapped mountains of Colorado," I felt only space and possibility and light. I knew that this vision could not have come from my limited perspective and consciousness; therefore, I deduced that it could only have come from God.

Our time together continued for another hour and a half, the cheap recorder hissing on the table. "Spirit's" orientations came to me through Marguerite: that one day I would work in a more holistic school, that I would follow a spiritual path that encompassed many cultures, and that someday I would use my voice as an instrument to call upon God. I allowed these images to augment my perspective of what was ahead of me in life, and after giving Marguerite fifty dollars in cash, I began to gather my things and head back to the material world. Marguerite had returned to herself, her posture that of a housewife and mother, her voice softer, rounded.

We said our goodbyes and shared a hug. "I'll keep you posted on my job search," I added, but after the quizzical look on her face, I realized that Marguerite remembered nothing from the previous hour and a half—just as she had informed me at the beginning of our session. Perhaps she cleaned up the crumbs on the kitchen table or helped her daughter with her homework after I left. I drove away from the grand old trees, illuminated, grateful, and feeling very small in comparison to the universe revealed to me.

And now, almost three years later on the floating bridge, I pop the cassette into the tape deck, prepared to rewind and fast-forward to find the section where Marguerite spoke of my work with holistic education; perhaps there will be some details that can assist us with forming a charter school. After pressing the play button and adjusting the volume, I sit back, held firmly in my seat by the sound of her powerful "channeling" voice as it resonates throughout the car. "Your kindred spirit are in the snowcapped mountains of Colorado."

I imagine the ringing of one of those old-fashioned alarm clocks sounding off right next to my ear. Even though there is no such thing in my car, my entire body responds to Marguerite's words as if it were so. My eyes open wide, mouth drops open with a quick exhalation, and shoulders slump with the sudden awareness—my time in the Pacific Northwest is over!

I nod my head in affirmation, ready to obey. Seconds later, a car horn honks behind me. The traffic has started to move. Shifting into drive as quickly as I can, I glance at the license plate of the car in front of me as it pulls forward. It has Colorado plates, white mountains against a green background—there's no stopping now.

CHAPTER TWELVE

THE VOICE

"Okay God, where is my spiritual family? I'll go anywhere!" I pleaded out loud, sitting in front of the altar on my bedroom floor.

It had been weeks since that moment on the floating bridge when I heard Marguerite's voice ringing through my stereo, telling me that my kindred spirit were in the snowcapped mountains of Colorado, but I had not yet been able to assimilate her vision into my physical world. I was feeling stuck teaching at school every day. I was spending my free time in a relationship with a nice enough man, but it wasn't going anywhere. We had different values and aspirations, and I didn't like wasting my time.

And it didn't help my mood that the spring rains were going on and on, forming much-dreaded "black ice" on the roads.

So I sat and meditated stubbornly, prepared to wait—all night if I had to—until I received an answer about what I was supposed to do in order to find my kindred spirit. After all, Colorado was a large state—where would I even begin? Moving to a densely populated city such as Denver, for example, was not a palatable option for me, nor was finding a job in another public school system. I was a few months shy of turning thirty, and all I sensed in front of me was a vast emptiness, a question mark.

Frustrated, I called out my question in the candlelit room. Once the vibration of my voice wafted out of the room, the silence answered me: "Go to Telluride."

"Where?" I snapped my head over my right shoulder toward the sleet-splattered window.

"Go to Telluride," the silence repeated firmly.

I am going to take a moment here to explain how I heard this voice, for this would not be the only time in my life I would receive information in this manner. The voice did not come from outside of me into my ear; rather, it bloomed inside my head, sprung from deep in my core, the shape and weight of the words leaving an impression in my mind that could not be erased.

"Oh!" I exclaimed. What could I make of this response? I whispered the unfamiliar word "Telluride" over and over again, feeling its curve on my tongue, a puzzle piece with unexplored nooks.

It was a final answer; nothing more would come that night, so I crawled into bed and slept straight through until morning when the gray April light slipped through the blinds. I could still feel the impression and vibration of the words "Go to Telluride" in the upper right side of my head as I got out of bed, walked into the living room, and turned on the television. As I crossed the room toward the kitchen, the words of the TV reporter on *Good Morning America* followed me, "Reporting live from Telluride, Colorado ..."

"What?" I croaked and turned toward the TV once again.

There on the screen was a bird's-eye view of the snowcapped mountains of Telluride, set against a blazing, blue sky. It was reported that the supermodel Christie Brinkley had been in a heli-skiing accident. The helicopter crashed and left five skiers stranded at high altitude, though fortunately everyone had been rescued and was doing fine.

"Wow, there really is a Telluride," I thought, connecting the TV footage with last night's meditation. And it's in the snow-capped mountains of Colorado! I shook my head free of the wild images of spruce trees on blue-white snow.

Later that day, at my beloved Stone House Bookstore, I purchased a guidebook for the state of Colorado. From the couple of brief paragraphs about Telluride, I learned that it was a ski town (which I wasn't very interested in) at 8,750 feet in elevation where it snowed approximately eight months out of the year (which I was also not very interested in). Located in the San Juan mountains in southwestern Colorado, its year-round population was only about 1,000. None of these facts sat well with me. It was cold, snowy, remote, and had few people; it didn't sound very appealing, or practical for that matter.

With a disappointed shrug, I set aside the book and the previous night's response to my plea. You might wonder how I could do that—set aside that intuition, that silent voice that spoke through the sleet.

It's easy. I was tired—tired after three years of waking up in the predawn hours to the rain-soaked Douglas firs and slogging my way through seven classes in a deteriorating school climate before driving home in the dark twilight, the day all but gone. And I was unsure. I thought I had always known what was best for me, but on the precipice of my fourth decade, my inner landscape had notably changed. I longed for a quieter life, for time in nature, for ritual and dreams. My conducting and teaching career didn't seem to fit. I was afloat.

But the mountains of Colorado were still firmly in front of me, tantalizing, challenging—Did I dare?—Seattle fading in the rearview mirror. I would have to close my life in Seattle, including leaving my position at Evergreen Junior High. It was a big decision to make.

Having doubts about whether or not I should, indeed, quit my job, I once again sat down at my altar and said, "Okay, God, I want to know if it's time for me to leave my job, and please, give me a really big sign!" I wanted to be sure.

After sitting for some moments in silence and hearing nothing, I gave up and went to bed.

Early the next morning, I had a dream that I was standing on my podium in front of my fifty-two-member, seventh-grade band, conducting a rehearsal. I was waving my arms as they worked their way laboriously, and loudly, through a piece. To my right, I saw the band room door swing open, my vice principal striding through. She approached me and, reaching up, tapped me on the shoulder. With a grand cutoff, I stopped the band, fragments of melody falling around us, and turned to her.

"It's time for you to go now," she said clearly, solemnly, her wide blue eyes peering up through wire-framed glasses.

The memory of last night's request for a "really big sign" superimposed itself into my dream state. I paused and breathed in the entirety of the band room, my kids' faces, the heat of their fifty-two bodies, the scent of school lunch filtering through the door.

I looked up at the ceiling, fist raised in victory, and said, "Thank you, God, for that clear answer!"

The following afternoon, I drafted my letter of resignation. How could I convey the surging movement of the waters within me through the dot-matrix computer printer? I came to the conclusion that I couldn't, so I kept it simple—it was time to move on. After the last rehearsal of the day, I stood before my principal as she accepted my letter, nodded my thanks, and left her office, the sound of a distant river calling me home.

On the last day of school in June, a dreary, drizzly, yet warm, day, I dressed carefully, wearing my medicine bag in public for the first time. It was given to me by Marguerite before my departure for Seattle three years earlier. She called me one night— Spirit had told her that I would be "relocating soon"—and said that she had to teach me some things before I left. We spent an evening among the pungent herbs in her apothecary, where she taught me how to build an altar and honor the full moon. She didn't remember her words about the snowcapped mountains of Colorado from our channeling session, and I didn't say anything. I knew that I must first go to Seattle; a good job offer was the sign I had been looking for, and I had a relationship there to see through. Colorado would wait.

Now I brought my students—one band at a time—to a grassy hillside near the parking lot. We formed a circle and said our goodbyes; I blessed each one of them with tobacco, sprinkling a few grains on each of their heads, saying their individual strengths and gifts out loud. My last group was my beloved band that had stayed with me for all three years; we smiled through our tears mixed with the rain on our faces and they gave me gifts for my road trip to the Southwest—a used Wispa Lite stove, a canister of gas, an address book with their names and addresses filled in, beautiful cards expressing their love and appreciation for the years we had spent together. We hugged in the rain, arms around each other as we climbed the hill back to our classroom.

At the end of the day, I turned in my final report cards and band room keys, said goodbye to the folks in the front office, and drove down Union Hill for the last time.

CHAPTER THIRTEEN

PORT ORFORD

O n July 3, 1994, I left Redmond in my Suzuki with a duffle bag full of clothes, a tent, a backpack, and camping supplies—including the Wispa Lite stove from my students. My entire summer salary was already in the bank, plus extra pay for all of the sick days that I did not use during my tenure at Evergreen. If I was careful, it was enough money for a few months of travel before I would need to settle down and start earning a paycheck again. I had ended the lease early on my apartment in Redmond, leaving behind the swimming pool and Douglas firs and stowing my couch, futon, and other belongings into a small storage unit down the road. I was free to do whatever I wanted to do, to go wherever my intuition and dreams led me.

I cruised down Route 101, driving a leisurely thirty-five miles an hour, passing through one small beach town after another, sampling fresh fish, raspberries, and chocolate malts. I rode with the windows open to the salt air and made my way slowly down the state with the goal of spending the night in Port Orford with some friends.

I reached my friend's, Karen and Joe's, home late that night and was greeted warmly. A kind, older man who rode a Harley, Joe and I had completed our first vision quests together. It was his feather earring I had worn the entire previous year, a gift that I snagged shamelessly when he decided to give away many of his material possessions. Over a late dinner of cornbread and chili, we caught up on the happenings of our lives, laughing at the gusty winds that pushed their way through the window screens; I commented on the deliciousness of the fresh air, and Joe joked, "Yeah, there's just too much of it!"

We finished the evening by candling each other's ears—a first for me. I loved the feeling of having wax drawn out of my ears, lying on my side with a paper plate on my head, ready to catch any errant drips from the paper candle which was burning only inches from my hair. Afterward, I was able to hear the slightest rustling of air and the lapping of the Elk River below, my ears as sensitive as those of a newborn. Karen and Joe tucked me into a large teepee on the front lawn, layering me in blankets, where I fell into a deep sleep as the wind billowed up into the night, whispering, "Sleep in peace, sleep in peace."

The next day was the Fourth of July, and the whole town gathered for the annual "Jubilee" parade, featuring girls on horseback throwing saltwater taffy and decorated tractors. I ended up on a float with Karen, waving a flag at the feisty crowds. Later, we joined the locals for fish and chips and, of course, fireworks, giggling like kids and "oohing" and "aahing" as orange and blue streams spread across the sky.

Some fifteen years later, I would unwittingly stumble into this charming town once again with my husband, Peter, and daughter, Ellen, on our way to visit Peter's brother, Johnny, who was stricken with multiple sclerosis (MS) and living in Eugene. Driving north on Route 101 into town, I would be shocked at the sense of familiarity until after some moments of reflection I realized where I was and remembered my first visit in 1994.

Excited to share a bit of history with my family, I suggested we stay the night. We found a one-star hotel—yes, they really do exist—that was clean enough, and we ate fish and chips at the same restaurant (The Crazy Norwegian's Fish & Chips!) I had fifteen years earlier. Later that evening, with Peter snoring next to me and Ellen dreaming beneath a head of unbrushed hair, I listened to the billowing winds once again and sent a message on them to my younger self, saying, "Sleep in peace, sleep in peace."

CHAPTER FOURTEEN

NEVADA SONG

The canyon I pulled into in central Nevada was dry and colorless, but at the hour nearing sunset, the diffuse light gracefully tinted the canyon walls varying shades of tan, butter, and mauve. I had mistakenly left my windows and vents open as I climbed the forest service road, making a mess of the inside of my car; it would be weeks before I could clean the dust from the crevices around my stereo, but I contentedly set up camp under some brush oak near a tiny stream.

No one else was around, as this was not a regular campground. More often than not I preferred being isolated. I enjoyed hearing only the sounds of nature, the rustling of the dry trees, the wind skirting the canyon above, or the flap of a raven's wings—"hwa, hwa, hwa"—overhead. I settled my back against a large cottonwood, nestling into the sandy earth, and took out my soprano wooden recorder to see if I could imitate and improvise with the hum around me. I was on my way to Bryce Canyon in the next few days and knew that I would find a Native American flute in one of the trading posts nearby, but for the moment, I had to make do with the soprano recorder.

A minor key is the closest you can get to imitating the sound of wind as the night approaches, and only five pitches are really necessary. Do, me (a flat third), fa, sol, and te (flat seventh) do a nice job of rising plaintively above the trees and blending with the vibration of a slow, running creek over wide, flat rocks. I played on and on, enjoying adding my own tune to the landscape as the sun dipped behind the canyon wall, the colors becoming muted and fuzzy, until something low to the ground moved to my left.

I had never seen a large snake before, only a few garter snakes while hiking in the Cascades of Washington, but I didn't panic when my eyes focused on this beauty, his head rising a couple of feet above his coiled body.

"Ho, Grandfather," I instinctively said, paying homage and bowing my head, not wanting to threaten him. I waited for him to do something—rattle, attack me, move on—but he just regarded me coolly, as if to say, "Well, you called me here."

He didn't seem aggressive in the least, so I returned my recorder to my lips and began playing again. Entranced, the snake remained for some moments, and we enjoyed the evening breeze together until, finally, as the light faded, he turned his head and slithered back to his place for the night. Admittedly, I was relieved and quickly decided to sleep in my dusty car, high off the ground, rather than my more spacious tent in order to avoid another late-night visitor.

CHAPTER FIFTEEN

NATIVE FLUTE

Well into the second week of July, the heat was extreme, but it was bearable because it was so dry. As folks say, "It's not the heat, it's the humidity"—accent on the "yum-ID-ity." I flew across Nevada into southern Utah at about eighty miles an hour, windows open to the sauna-like weather, still hoping that the remaining Nevada dust would clear out of my car. My destination was Bryce Canyon National Park. I don't know how that destination got into my head. Perhaps one of my Evergreen students or parents mentioned it to me as a "must-see," but it had become an almost mystical place to me as I was planning my itinerary the previous month. More importantly, I knew that I would find the perfect Native American flute in a trading post along the way.

When I mentioned this to Marguerite from a pay phone in Newport, Oregon, she had said, "Ah yes, you will be transmitting Spirit through this flute, but someday you will do it with your voice instead," leaving me with the sense that, indeed, this too would come to pass as had all of Marguerite's visions. She seemed to reach deep into my consciousness and pull out the most light-filled, sparkly dreams that had not yet risen to my awareness and place them in front me like beacons on my path, standing sentinels with an air of, "Of course, this is what you are meant to become."

Between Panguitch and Hatch, Utah, on Highway 12, there was a trading post that carried the usual native crafts—blankets, jewelry, and knickknacks. I strolled through the store, enjoying the opportunity to stretch my legs, and made my way toward the back, feeling that this would be the place where I encountered my flute. Not seeing any evidence of a flute, my mood sank as I examined the fringed blankets, pretending to be interested in finding just the right color combination. But as I rounded the corner, I spied a display case with exactly what I was looking for: several modestly priced flutes, just enough of a selection for me to know that one of them would be perfect.

The middle-aged native man behind the counter was gracious, his head bowing each time I asked to try one more flute. I appreciated his quiet manner as he gave me the space to play the scale on each instrument and discover what it had to say. The second flute I tried had already captivated me with its soft tone, minor scale, and clear, light upper octave, but I went on to try a few more in the name of being thorough.

Returning to the second flute, I played a simple, improvised melody, not unlike the song that had captivated the snake back in Nevada. I nodded to the man and his eyes glimmered in accord. One hundred and forty dollars later, the flute and its fringed case were now an extension of me.

CHAPTER SIXTEEN

THE WATERS WITHIN

I t was finally time to find out what Bryce Canyon had to tell me. I headed toward the visitor center, along with a couple days' worth of groceries, to get my back-country permit. The ranger at the visitor center kindly showed me on the map where I could park my car at the end of a dirt road in order to access the twenty-two-mile Under-the-Rim Trail that would take me to my camping area for the night. It was already evening, just a couple of hours before sunset, when I finally arrived at the access point, parking against the flimsy fence.

Considering how long I had been planning and looking forward to getting into Bryce Canyon, I was feeling unenthusiastic about hauling my loaded-down backpack into the woods and setting up camp as evening fell. I procrastinated my departure for a while, eating a sandwich, then some chips, then finishing off my Coke, reasoning that it would be better if I didn't have to carry as much food.

By the time I brushed my teeth and tidied up the backseat of my car, the sun had already set, the surrounding woods grown still. Not wanting to fight inertia any longer, I settled back into the front seat and stared dully past the small, grassy field into the now dark woods, finally admitting to myself that I would not enter them this evening. I was hypnotized by my surroundings, simply obeying their orders to stay put; there was no rush to go anywhere that night. My job was to encounter what awaited within.

Before long, the first-quarter moon had risen, casting a gossamer, dreamlike quality both inside my thoughts and outside my windows. Not wanting to turn on my car, I lost awareness of time as I floated, trancelike, into a meditative state. Invisible hands kept me still, not moving or thinking about what I might do next. None of this was about doing; after years of doing, doing, doing, I was sinking into myself, into being, stilling my cells down to my eyelashes so that I could attend to something deeper.

Like the movement of water far below the frozen surface of a lake, I was being drawn downward to the river inside of me and all that had been recorded there, and when I finally descended deep enough, I reached out to touch what was there. As the light of my awareness illuminated the watery depths, a roiling reaction quaked through my entire body. Snapping out of my meditation, I felt fear seeping into my eyes and thoughts, creating a filter as I looked toward the meadow and the woods beyond it.

Something was lurking out there, waiting for me. Only the confines of my car would keep me safe, so I hurriedly rolled up my windows, shutting out the cool air, reaching across and behind the seats to lock the doors, my breath quickening, restricted. Staring through my windshield into the dim moonlight, I couldn't see anything—no movement, no shadow, no depth. I sat there, paralyzed, waiting as fear tingled through each part of my body, setting me on edge.

As the time passed, an urgency arose within me: I had to pee, the Coke from hours earlier making its presence known. There was no way I was leaving the car, so I continued my vigil, hoping that the feeling would pass, listening for movement or an intuition as to what I was supposed to do—but nothing came. The gentle sounds of nature on a summer night, the breezes that might have blown or the owls that might have hooted companionably, could not penetrate the wall of fear that had thickened inside of me. I sat alone, hardening.

But like the constant trickle of water beneath the frozen stream, my bladder had filled beyond discomfort into a throbbing ache, and I wrestled with the fact that I could no longer deny my need. Like a child running to the bathroom in the middle of the night, I swung my door open, pants pulled down, and squatted to relieve myself, not daring to look beyond the wedges of metal protecting me on two sides. Seconds later, I hopped back into the car, slamming the door and hunching down in the front seat so that no one and nothing could see me. My breath shallow, eyes cast downward, I retreated once again into myself until, spent and weary, I passed into a dark and silent sleep.

I dreamt that the dawn light filtered through my open windows. I felt a presence, unidentifiable, seated next to me in the passenger seat.

"I am sorry I abused you," it said. The words came from eons ago, across a lifetime.

Soothed, I nodded as the fabric within adjusted, quelling the anxiety that had taken up residence in my waters. I closed my eyes for a moment, my insides unwrinkled, newly smooth, and when I reopened them, the presence was gone like a vapor that had slipped through the now-closed car windows. The grasses in the meadow were undulating in the early morning breeze, greeting a new day in Bryce Canyon, the air fresh and soft.

Without another thought, I turned the key in the ignition and drove back toward the highway.

CHAPTER SEVENTEEN

AN OLD HORSE

A fter two weeks of passing through desert-brown scenery, my eyes were craving a bit of green, but before I could get to southwestern Colorado, I had to cross into northeastern Arizona, then up to the Four Corners area on Route 160, which would eventually take me through Cortez and on to Durango, my destination for the next week or so. Having left Bryce Canyon in the rearview mirror, I felt tired and dusty, but peaceful, as if all of the knots inside of me had been untied. My breath expanded easily in the hot afternoon air, and my mind was curiously, and blessedly, empty. There was nothing to latch onto in this arid landscape, mentally or visually, so I simply kept my eyes on the road as I wended my way through the Navajo and Ute reservations in silence.

I didn't have any music that matched my blank mood or the colorless background bleached by the midday sun, and that was fine by me. The final notes of my Evergreen band students had dissipated from my neural pathways many weeks earlier, and I reveled in the quiet spaces that had revealed themselves in recent days. F-naturals where there should have been F-sharps had routinely formed a backdrop in my thoughts for the past three years, and I wondered what would now take up that space, though I was not in a rush to find out.

Less than an hour west of Durango, pops of dark, lush green appeared sporadically between the red rocks, awakening my senses to the changing landscape. As I began to climb into the La Plata mountains, entering ponderosa pine country and more rarified air, I found myself refreshed as if rising from a long nap, my thoughts quickening as the traffic thickened. I recognized the Four Winds motel on Route 160 just outside of Durango, but since I was on a budget, I pulled into the Lightner Creek campground and gladly rented a cabin for the next week.

Two months earlier in May, I had made a brief jaunt to Durango to participate in a seminar called "Domain Shift." It was one of those workshops where you essentially spend most of the time dancing, hyperventilating (at least I did, due to the altitude), screaming, and beating pillows in order to become emotionally clear of your past. This was a new concept for me, and I admit I gained something from it. After four days of reliving our worst memories, which could include anything from abuse to being the last one picked for the kickball team in gym class, we were taught and encouraged—to literally move out our anger, fear, and frustration, our unfortunate hotel pillows on the receiving end. I hadn't realized how much of that pent-up emotional goo was inside of me, and I found it easily accessible, especially when surrounded by fourteen other people who were intently beating on their hotel pillows, too.

At the end of each seminar day, I returned to the Four Winds motel, about a twenty-five-minute drive from the private home north of the city where our seminar took place. My drive took me through the heart of Durango and, blessedly, past an Arby's restaurant where there were two roast beef and cheddar sandwiches waiting for me every night. The vegetarian fare served at "Domain Shift" didn't cut the mustard in my estimation; this was hard work, and only a sizeable portion of fat and carbs would sustain me. Flopping on the bed and turning on the television, the smell of French fries would fill the room where I rested until the next day's screaming and pillow-beating.

On the last day of the seminar, our group leaders led us through an exercise imagining what it would be like to reenter our current lives. They explained in great detail the conflicts that awaited us, the lack of understanding that would be shown to us, and encouraged us to dig deeply into our discomfort with the reality of going home. I tried my best but really couldn't come up with anything and, feeling inadequate, decided to take a break out on a deck that faced some private woods.

Staring into the ponderosas, I concentrated my attention deep in my belly—surely there must be something frightening in there. As I breathed in, I felt a movement—ah, there it is!

After forcing my breath downward in an attempt to root out the offending emotion, a large bubble of sound escaped my mouth.

Horrified, I realized that I wasn't afraid of going home. I was very much looking forward to it, and my relief at this knowledge was cascading out of me in peals of laughter. I clamped my hand over my mouth; I felt guilty laughing while everyone else inside had gone back to their screaming and pillow-beating. But then I thought, "Wait a minute—this is what I'm here for," and I uncovered my mouth and roared heartily into the woods, my belly full of roast beef and cheddar sandwiches. I laughed until I cried, so when I entered the house a few minutes later, I looked like everyone else—red-faced, tear-streaked, blown out. It was the end of our four days together, and after saying my sincere thanks and goodbyes, I drove once more through the heart of Durango knowing that I would be back someday.

Two months later, the cabin at the Lightner Creek campground was rustic and cozy—a bed, a nightstand, and a screened window through which I saw my first hummingbirds, a pair of them about as large as my thumb gazing in the window while I unpacked. This was a civilized place with clean bathrooms nearby and families laughing as they hit up the vending machine for chips and candy bars. At sixteen dollars a night, it was the perfect spot from which to explore Durango during the next week.

You might be wondering at this point why I was in Durango when only three months earlier the voice of God had told me quite clearly to go to Telluride. One of my favorite books is Natalie Goldberg's *Long Quiet Highway*, a memoir in which, in one part, she compares people and their rates of waking up spiritually to horses. Some people are quicker and need very little prodding to get on their way, but others are like an old horse that needs to be kicked repeatedly to get moving. I would like to think of myself as a responsive horse, and there have been times in my life when my actions would qualify, but this wasn't one of those times.

I had quieted the voice and its clear direction with thoughts such as, "It's too cold in Telluride—too remote, too small—and I don't like to ski." Besides, I reasoned further, Durango was a college town and it might have more job opportunities, and it's only a two-hour drive from Telluride. Maybe God really meant for me to come here?

So, like a horse not quite out of the gate, I meandered through the streets of Durango that week, looking for signs that this was the place for me. I visited an alternative school north of town to see if there were any job openings, I drove up to the campus of Fort Lewis College and checked out the bulletin board outside of the music department, but no one was around during the height of summer break. There was only one movie playing in town, *Maverick*, which didn't interest me in the least.

From one day to the next I floated, aimless, not managing to connect with anyone in a meaningful way with the exception of a young woman named Rain who I had met in "Domain Shift" two months earlier. We visited in her A-frame cabin located just up the road from the campground, and I found myself envious that her parents had sent her to "Domain Shift" at such a young age. We ate grilled cheese sandwiches, and she told me how she had encountered a mountain lion on a recent hike, which endeared me to the Durango area even less.

After a week of not being able to penetrate my surroundings, I gave up, packed the car, and drove an hour east to Pagosa Springs for a "break." I was exhausted by the abrupt change from having a daily routine and an apartment to being on the road, wandering from one place to another, from one moment to the next. Pagosa Springs boasted a number of hot springs, some of them commercialized catering to tourists, others tucked into the hills, only reachable by a hike of two or three miles.

I parked my tent in a campground just outside of town and set out around noon the next day to hike up the mountain and find one of the more remote springs. I had scant verbal directions given to me by the campground attendant and a bottle of Snapple iced tea—what more did I need? Hiking upward on an old logging road, I passed people who were already coming down and took the opportunity to refine my directions. The day was warm and sunny, and I felt carefree as I climbed higher. But as anyone with any mountain experience knows—and I did not qualify as someone who had any mountain experience or I would have taken more with me than a bottle of Snapple iced tea—the weather can change abruptly on a summer afternoon in July. The monsoon pattern had come in what appeared to be about a minute and a half, and as I was reaching the top of the hill after two hours of hiking, the sky opened up into a downpour with gusting winds, thunder, and lightning.

I took cover in a stand of ponderosas, my t-shirt and shorts already soaked through, before I noticed a small tent hidden behind the thick scrub oak. Hovering underneath the rain fly was a small man, gnomelike with a long, blond beard and piercing blue eyes, staring right at me, motionless. I waved in an attempt to appear brave and said a soft "Hi," my greeting muffled by the rainfall still pounding down. He nodded softly, rose to his feet, and was standing by my side within seconds.

Despite my New Jersey upbringing, which rang a loud alarm in my head that this man was probably an axe murderer, I found myself enjoying an honest conversation with this gentle soul who was on a sort of a quest, living in solitude until all of his past trauma had leaked into the earth, leaving him clean and ready to return to society. He shared all of this in our first two minutes of conversation—not your typical trail talk—and I could totally relate. When the rain slowed from hard bullets to a calm drizzle, the thunder retreating, he showed me to the hot springs only yards away, and we stripped down to nothing, easing ourselves into the sulfuric water. I didn't care that I was naked in front of a strange man. I had nothing to hide, and he kept a respectful distance. We leaned our heads back, the rain plopping on our foreheads, its velocity slowing as it passed through the trees above.

We soaked and soaked, and I found myself finally relaxing after weeks of driving and wandering around the Southwest, a silence opening up inside me that was soon matched by the still air. The rain had stopped, and all we had was time—time to regard the thinning clouds and the blades of grass as they slowly sprang up while the rain evaporated, time to dig and curl our toes, rooting into the muddiness of the hot springs, time to drop the shoulders and be measured within nature at its own pace until the moment we climbed out, skin wrinkled. I air-dried as I stepped into my shorts and tossed on my t-shirt. The man graciously filled my empty Snapple bottle from his water stash and pointed me back down the mountain.

Nothing looked the same on the way down. The logging road had become a river, so I picked my way through the mud on the side, rivulets of water rushing into my boots, the squelching sounds replacing the silence. It was a different kind of music. Silence allows for all kinds of possibility, whereas squelching focused me on the task at hand: get down the mountain as quickly as possible, for the sun had already set and it would soon be dark. The threat of running into a mountain lion motivated me to descend even more quickly, breaking into a half-run until I finally saw my car at the trailhead just before it was enclosed in darkness.

CHAPTER EIGHTEEN

BLACK CANYON

The wind whipped around like a disobedient child, my tent its mischievous sibling, slipping out of my hands every time I tried to drive the tent stake into the rocky soil. I had been struggling to set up camp for fifteen minutes, sand gusting into my mouth and eyes, the wind so strong it seemed to suck the air right out of my nostrils.

It was a hot afternoon at the campground in the Black Canyon of the Gunnison, and no one else was around—not a welcoming sign. Even the name "Black Canyon" wasn't warm and fuzzy. In that moment, however, it was an apt description of my mood—dark and bottomless—for I had been on the road for about a week

91

after leaving Pagosa Springs without a clear goal, wondering if I had made a big mistake in leaving my life in Seattle.

I had driven south into New Mexico toward Taos. I was imagining that I would magically run into Natalie Goldberg on the street while visiting an art gallery and purchasing great bunches of roasted chili peppers, as she had spent a significant part of her life there under that expansive, knock-your-socks-off blue sky. But after sitting in rush-hour traffic for more than a few minutes, I was circling back out north of town when I noticed a small sign off the highway that simply said "Lama" with an arrow pointing east up a graveled road.

A spiritual community formed in 1967, the Lama Foundation was open to anyone who wanted to spend some time there, so I drove up the road through the woods, parked in the designated lot, and walked the remainder of the way. I spent just one night, helping out in the kitchen and meditating in the evening and early morning, trying to find my center and reconnect with the purpose of this trip.

Still feeling restless, I left the next day, this time driving north to Denver to visit my cousin, Mandi, and her husband, Larry, who had just moved to Colorado that same year. We spent two days catching up and enjoying each other's company, but despite the familial warmth that I felt during our visit, I couldn't ignore my discomfort from being back in a large city. I felt a constant tug from southwestern Colorado. After a month of traveling, I still had not explored Telluride, which my conscience reminded me of every moment. It was time to go, so I left Denver on a Tuesday morning, July 26, and headed through the central part of the state over Monarch Pass. I reasoned that since it was a long drive to Telluride, I would spend the night at the halfway point in the Black Canyon of the Gunnison.

And so I found myself wrestling with my uncooperative tent. Each time I managed to drive one tent stake into the unyielding soil, another one would pop out and the wind would catch the entire tent, thrusting it upward. I finally gave up and sat down in the rocky sand with my head in my hands, the words tumbling out of my mouth of their own volition, "I don't want to be here—I want to be in Telluride!"

Suddenly I felt clear for the first time in weeks, back on track and ready to move forward. Gathering my wayward tent into my arms and rolling it up, I stuffed it into the back of my car, sand flying everywhere. I slammed the hatch closed and jumped into the driver's seat, turning the key and gunning the gas pedal—I couldn't get out of there fast enough.

Three and a half hours later, after climbing over Dallas Divide, then driving down into a canyon along the San Miguel river, I ascended one last time and entered the box canyon where the jewel that is Telluride sits. At 6 p.m., everyone was out on the main street, promenading and socializing, the sun streaming toward the east end of town, lighting up the canyon with its "alpine glow." Creeping along at fifteen miles per hour allowed me to see the smiling faces, the many dogs, and the marquee of the Nugget movie theatre, which to my great thrill was playing a foreign film—a foreign film! That meant educated people lived here! I continued cruising through town toward the town park where I could find a campsite for the night.

Once in the park I discovered that no sites were available, but a kind man named John allowed me to pitch my tent in his site. Slightly embarrassed, I extracted my tent from the back of my car, still balled up from hours earlier, shook it out, and within moments had it assembled. I was eager to explore the town on foot, so after a bit of small talk and a sincere thank you to John for sharing his campsite, I grabbed my wallet and left the town park.

Walking up the sunny side of main street (it's real name is Colorado Ave.), I eased my way through the groups of locals and tourists alike heading out to dinner or to the movies or hanging out on benches enjoying the summer evening, their bicycles and dogs nearby. I couldn't help but smile broadly at anyone who made eye contact, which included just about everyone I passed. They smiled back at me, nodding a friendly hello. Joyous, my feet floated softly up the street in the direction of the sun, which was sitting low in the sky. I didn't know where I was going; I only knew I desperately wanted to explore the unfamiliar streets of this mountain town before it got too dark.

Moments later, I found myself on the east side of the Elk's building, which at that time was located next to a small park called Elk's Park. Standing in front of Eddie's Pizza, I gazed across the street to the north. And this was when everything changed, for what had been an unfamiliar townscape just seconds earlier was now a place sprung from deep in my memory.

The courthouse and the Sheridan Opera House stood to the north, a small plot of grass between them and a sidewalk along the Opera House headed farther north up the hill. I had ridden my bicycle on this very sidewalk three months earlier in a dream, my flute in my backpack on my way to teach a private lesson. I had all but forgotten this dream, for it had only lasted about five seconds, but it was enough time to firmly plant inside of me an image of Telluride that I would recognize months later—not only an image, but a sense of purpose, and most importantly, a feeling of home.

Standing outside of Eddie's Pizza, gazing at the very spot I had dreamt of, I felt my dream reach forward from the past and fill my eyes and heart, a future unfolding.

Looking up at the blue sky, I nodded and said out loud, "Yes, sir."

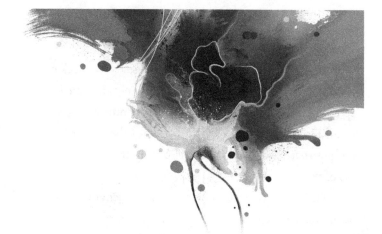

CHAPTER NINETEEN

MOVE TO TELLURIDE

W endy's friend, Jerry, held my palm with a curious look on his face. We were seated on her apartment floor on a sunny day in September of 1994 in Escondido, California. Having returned to Redmond for a few weeks in August, I was now moving to my new home in Telluride, my Suzuki Sidekick—purchased with four-wheel drive for the snowy conditions in Colorado—just outside the window in the parking lot, packed to the gills with all of my earthly belongings.

While back in Redmond, I made a few phone calls to people in Telluride who had been recommended to me by the owner of its local music store. If you want to find out what is going on in the music scene of any town, I suggest you check out the music store. This is where I went immediately after the moment I recognized Telluride from my dream. The music store was easy to find just a few blocks away and around the corner in an old building that used to be a brothel during the old-time mining days of yore.

"Oh, there isn't a music program in the schools, hasn't been one for years," the owner of the Telluride Music Company said, his head framed by the Martin guitars hanging on the wall behind him. "Sure, they used to have a great band program, but that dried up years ago. If you really want to know more about the music scene here, you ought to give Ulli a call."

And with that advice, I had my first conversation with Ulli, the beloved local piano teacher, a couple of weeks later. Upon hearing about my band-teaching background, Ulli exclaimed, "Ooh, I've been praying for someone like you to move to town for ten years now!" her thick German accent delighting my ears and bringing a smile to my face all the way in Seattle.

It was all the encouragement I needed to quickly wrap up my life, pack my car, and get going by mid-September. I wanted to arrive in Telluride before the equinox, and Ulli had kindly offered to host me until I found a place to rent (after making sure I had a four-wheel drive to handle the winter snows). I had also decided that, before settling in for the autumn and winter in Telluride, I would drive through southern California to visit my close friend, Wendy, in order to "fill up" on our brand of spiritual talk, beach time, and chocolate cupcakes.

I had met Wendy five years earlier at the University of Cincinnati in a women's spirituality group. At the group's first meeting, she approached me, a young woman with big hair and orange nail polish—the look of the late eighties. She bent toward me with earnest eyes and said, "Excuse me, can I tell you? You look just like my aunt!"

Thus, my friendship with Wendy had begun. It continued after the group meetings and weaved itself into my emerging spiritual path. She was only nineteen at the time but had already faced some significant challenges in her life and was well awakened to her spiritual nature. We meditated together, did tai chi in the park, and went to the New Age bookstore and read about crystals while eating corned beef from New Jersey that her mother would mail to her in vacuum-sealed packages.

Now settled in Escondido, Wendy chauffeured me amongst her metaphysical friends after we spent the day at a nearby beach.

"I see a man waiting for you in Telluride—a man and a little boy," Jerry prophesized, nodding his head in affirmation.

"Well, that was that," I thought to myself. I really wasn't interested in entering a new relationship, so I shrugged off his prediction and tossed it into a corner of my mind where it could rest for a while, alongside the astrologer's prediction (also a friend of Wendy's) two days earlier who had said the exact same thing. I simply didn't have the energy for that in my life. I had a whole new chapter to begin—students to recruit, flyers to make, a room to rent … you get the idea. I was about to manifest an entire life from the faint residue of a five-second dream, and I didn't have any time to spare.

CHAPTER TWENTY

PETER

As easily as a page is turned, I found myself in an entirely new setting. The steady drizzle and low-ceiling skies of Seattle, which had comprised my spiritual incubator for three years, were replaced by the crystalline blue mountain air, illuminated by never-ending sunshine. The thin air and light at an altitude of 8,750 feet has a clarity unlike any other, and I felt as if I were waking up from a long slumber, alert and focused. I had just turned thirty years old.

I arrived in Telluride at sunset on the autumnal equinox in 1994 and met up with Ulli in her cramped in-town studio. This would be the future home of many rehearsals together, with her upright piano and futon couch wedged between tall bookshelves stuffed with music.

In the encroaching darkness, I followed her up a dirt road on to the top of the mesa where she lived. We sang together—some of the songs were from my sweat-lodge experience—under the full moon out on the deck. What a wonderful thing to do when you first meet someone—sing a song! She invited me to join a group of women who were interested in forming an a capella group the following week. "You should join us!" she explained in her brusque accent, merrily pushing me to say "Yes, why not?"

I awoke the next day to my first expansive view of the San Juan mountains, including Wilson Peak. The aspen trees blazed gold against another impossibly blue sky, their last burst of warming color before the leaves would drop in the coming weeks. I marveled at the fact that instead of teaching at Evergreen Junior High School, or any school for that matter, I was poised on the edge of possibility, the broad vista like an empty page before me, accompanied by the bugling of elk and the chittering of fall foliage in the early morning breeze.

Fast-forward three weeks and I had already found a nice house to rent with amenable roommates and enrolled twenty-eight students into after-school woodwind and brass lessons. The principal of the school, a bearded and quiet-mannered man, allowed me to speak with these inquisitive, well-educated kids in their homeroom classes. I showed up with my feather earring and black Converse sneakers and offered my experience and vision of a student concert band. They left with my cheap flyers in their hands, chattering about which instruments they might want to take up. Their parents flooded me with phone calls, enthusiasm, and questions: "Where can we rent an instrument? Will my old clarinet work?"

Our classes began soon after, an alchemy of squeaks, honks, and laughter, from which eventually emerged recognizable tunes such as "Merrily We Roll Along" and "Lightly Row." Kids carrying trombones, alto saxes, and bell kits through the streets of Telluride became a common scene. I would run into their parents in the produce aisle of Rose Market, their faces earnest and warm.

I had also begun rehearsing with the lovely group of women Ulli had introduced me to. They had diverse backgrounds and a broad range of musical experience, from theatre to classical training to no formal training. They just wanted to sing for the joy of it. To this group, I added my low alto/tenor voice. Months later, one of the women quipped, "We don't need a male singer—we have Rhonda!"

For many years, week after week, we sang songs, stumbling through Ukrainian lyrics or pop tunes as we ate "potlucks, with five desserts!" our resident poet Rosemerry later wrote. We laughed and shared our stories. It was in this group that I formed some of my closest relationships during those early years in Telluride. Our name was Heartbeat.

One day I saw a flyer on the town kiosk advertising a five-week shamanic meditation class. I didn't have to think about it. It was a no-brainer, and I and signed up immediately. The first class would take place in just a few days, only steps away from my new home.

I arrived early on that first night of class, which was at the teacher's residence. After I introduced myself to the thirty-something man (a former tennis pro), I settled in on the leather couch and watched as other students filed in, sharing hugs, already familiar with each other, as is common in a town with a population of only a thousand or so.

I took in the scene, relaxed, and with a long and full inhale lifted my eyes to the door where a bearded, ponytailed man strode in, long-legged in faded Levi's and cowboy boots, illuminated by a large spotlight above his head.

Unbidden, a wave of emotion rose within me and my heart exclaimed of its own volition, "I am so happy to see him again!"

There wasn't really a light shining above him—at least not that anyone else could see—but within a time span of less than two seconds, the palm reader's and astrologer's prophecies crawled out of the corner where I had tossed them and were glittering in the air: "You are going to meet a man and a little boy."

And then, just as quickly, came a crash of disappointment as I saw that another woman was close behind, following him through the door. The spotlight had retreated behind the paneled walls.

"Oh no," I thought irrationally, "He's already with someone!"

From unbounded joy to muted despair, I shook my head as if to clear away a dream, took a deep breath, and raised my eyes once again to the rest of the room. I watched the bearded man as he took a seat to my right, the woman taking a seat far to my left, and it dawned on me that these two were not together. My heart cautiously opened, beaming at this man as we all introduced ourselves.

His name was Peter, and years later when I heard him recounting his perspective of this moment, he expressed his surprise as he wondered, "Who is this woman beaming at me and how do I know her?"

I futilely tried to follow instructions and meditate during the first hour of class, but my thoughts—and eyes—kept returning to this man. During the break, I approached Peter and told him I had just moved to Telluride, my story bubbling out of me, and invited him to sit with me for the remainder of the class. This was, again, not helpful to my meditation practice, as a current of electricity crackled between our knees only inches apart on the leather couch.

At the end of class, I tossed out an invitation to anyone interested, "Does anyone want to grab a bite to eat?"

Of course, the invitation was only meant for Peter, and I am grateful to this day that everyone else looked at their watches and muttered excuses about having to get up for work the next day or get back to their kids. They had all seen my unabashed interest in Peter throughout the class and kindly stepped aside so that we could get on within the flow of something that could not be stopped.

We ended up at Eddie's Pizza, only a few steps away from the sidewalk where, back in July, I had remembered the dream foretelling my time in Telluride. When I said, "Yes, sir," looking up to the blue, blue sky, this was part of what I was saying "yes" to.

I said "yes" to both the astrologer and the palm reader who predicted just weeks earlier that a man and a little boy were waiting for me. I said "yes" as we swapped life stories—Peter's significantly longer than mine since he is a full twenty years older than I. I said "yes" as he told me about his son, Eliot, who was only six years old. I said "yes" when he invited me to his cabin the following weekend, along with some other friends who never showed up because a winter storm was predicted, leaving us to our first night together of foot rubs and dancing to Barry White while Eliot slept soundly upstairs.

And exactly one year later, I said "yes" again at a wedding by a lake, surrounded by blazing aspen trees. As a raven and a red-tailed hawk joined paths directly in front of the late afternoon sun, I promised to follow Peter's long legs anywhere. Heartbeat sang, and my heart burst with joy as we danced the hora, me in a stained wedding dress that Eliot had spilled red wine on during the toast.

As an almost full moon rose over the mountains, Peter and Eliot set off an impressive show of fireworks with fits and starts, calling to each other as the colors reflected in our eyes and the darkened lake. We giggled "oohs" and "aahs" against the chill of the October night, inhaling the sharp air. I was both exhilarated and feeling deeply settled within myself. Who knew what would come, but I didn't doubt the forces that had brought me here to the snowcapped mountains of Colorado.

CHAPTER TWENTY-ONE

MOUNTAIN MUSIC

The chorus sang "O Sanctissima," more secularly known as the "Mariner's Hymn." Written in 1860, it calls on God to save "those in peril on the sea." In the snowcapped mountains of Colorado, our adult community choir—an integral part of the newly formed Telluride Choral Society—was as far from the sea as we could get, and since our December WinterSing concerts were upon us, we rehearsed the Latin/Christmas version of the original hymn.

I was happily ensconced in the tenor section in the second pew of Christ Church, just one of a sixty-or-so-member choir that rehearsed on Wednesday evenings under the direction of a young, charismatic, and talented conductor, John Yankee. The world of choral music was opening up to me once again, having lain dormant in my life since my years in the Women's Glee Club at MSU. Every Wednesday evening I learned about shaping vowels and blend and the classical repertoire of the choral world, which was substantially different from the earthy and contemporary sounds of the concert band repertoire.

On weekday mornings, I stretched into downward dog and plow pose as I looked up the valley at the sun rising over the box canyon. Then I spent some time rehearsing my parts, whether they were of the more classical nature for the Telluride Choral Society or of the more folk (or sometimes banal) nature for Heartbeat. Afternoons were spent with my brass and woodwind groups, their honks and squeaks gradually progressing into characteristic band sounds as autumn turned into winter.

Winters are long at 8,750 feet in altitude. From November to April six to eight inches of fresh snow covered the potholes in Telluride almost every morning. I bought my first, and only, pair of Sorels for 120 dollars, so I could stomp through every kind of terrain in the local "fashion." No leather pumps for these hardy mountain folks! Should a dress-up occasion come to pass, our winter boots were acceptably paired with our black, velvet dresses—or, for men, jackets and bolo ties.

Evenings were spent in rehearsals of various types. Since I was one of only a few professionally trained musicians, I was put to good use singing in the Telluride Choral Society's Chorale, singing in the more experienced Chamber Singers, or playing the flute in the Chamber Orchestra or pit orchestra for the local theatre company. In the ensuing years, I would even form a wind ensemble, one player to a part, and revisit the Holst "Suite" in E-flat and Per-sichetti's "Pageant." I enjoyed the warmth and laughter of fellow musicians, our mutual respect, and the variety of music that we experienced together. I filled one black binder after another with new music from each ensemble, alphabetizing and labeling each one. More than twenty years later, their labels are faded but still legible—pop, jazz, classical, folk, Heartbeat, and so on.

I was happy and fulfilled, but as many independent musi-cians can attest, happiness doesn't always add up in one's check-ing account. Income from private teaching and gigs is subject to the ebb and flow of students on summer vacation or grant funding to support a local production. I was operating "in the red," a situation that was less than comfortable for a thirty-some-thing-year-old.

Coincidentally, the local public school district was finally ready to develop its general music and band program after not having one for many years. My checkbook balance, along with the desire to have a home and grow mine and Peter's family someday, provided the force for me to, once again, compose a new resume and drop it off at the school. Even though I had left Seattle with thinking, "I am never going to teach in a public school again," here I was, unemotionally calculating my material future. Returning to a reliable source of income simply added up. I was immediately hired to teach general music and begin-ning band at the start of the next school year.

Out came the magic markers once again as I made rhythm flashcards for my students. Sheet music was stuffed into fold-ers for my band students, posters were hung, recorders were ordered, and pencils were sharpened.

Even now, after more than thirty years of teaching, I still get excited about the beginning of the school year. I love how the kids get out their instruments after not having played for an entire summer and set their lips to mouthpieces with stiff, new reeds, laughing at the horrific noises that come out at first. I love how we plow our way through new music, feet tapping, the kids' eyes wide in disbelief as they listen to a professional recording of the music that sits on their stands. "We can't possible play that!" they exclaim, but with only weeks of dogged effort, you can hear the music finally breaking through.

Once again, my life neatly fit into a routine of bells ringing, my room filling and emptying with kids from kindergarten through middle school banging rhythms on drums, blowing (way too forcefully) into their recorders, or asking for a new reed. The scent of canned green beans and tater tots filtered into my room on the top floor of the old elementary school, as it was located right next to the teachers' lounge, and on stormy days, my students and I would watch the clouds moving up the canyon, bringing another six inches of fresh powder.

And so my first few years in Telluride were composed—each group I performed in or taught, a different song, each person I sang with and each student a different note that comprised the melodies. As a musician, a teacher, a conductor, a wife of Peter, and a stepmother to Eliot, I grew. After living in the snowcapped mountains of Colorado for five years, I had built a solid foundation musically, materially, and spiritually on which to explore a new role—that of being a mother.

CHAPTER TWENTY-TWO

MOTHERHOOD

In 1999, I was still teaching and performing full-time while my belly grew, my daughter, Ellen, rhythmically kicking her heel against my side during Chamber Singers' rehearsals. My fifth-grade students performed a song at their graduation in June, while my seven-month belly pushed against the portable keyboard I played during the ceremony. And every Wednesday afternoon, the a capella harmonies of Heartbeat swirled into the folds of my maternity blouses.

I dreamt of a little girl, redheaded, who followed me to all my rehearsals. A friend of mine dreamed that he could hear her

111

singing inside of me and saw her face pushed upward, imprinting itself in relief on my belly, her voice soaring outward.

After seven months of pregnancy, my attention turned inward. The school year was finished, and I had taken a maternity leave for the next year. The Choral Society season was over. Peter and I had purchased a log cabin on thirty-eight acres of land on a mesa, at the base of a dormant, volcanic mountain, some forty miles west of Telluride.

The music here was unlike any other in my life. It began with the awesome silence that we first experienced as Peter and I snowshoed across the meadow underneath a full moon after closing the deal the previous November. From the silence came the sound of snowfall striking the large, drafty living room windows throughout winter, along with the sound of the wind sailing in from the west, enveloping the ponderosa pines and aspen grove surrounding our cabin, a low-pitched whoosh underneath the higher crackle and pop of aspen logs burning in the fireplace.

In the spring, we heard the fresh-green song of tender aspen leaves as they turned in the breeze, alternating front and back, or the crunch of gravel as a neighbor drove down the one-third-mile driveway. At night, the howls of coyotes celebrating their wildness filled the air, and we laid cozily in bed, laughing uncontrollably as we discussed potential, awful names for our soon-to-be-born daughter, working our way through the alphabet—"gag reflex" and "hyperflangia." Peter, along with his years of medical training, has an unusually sharp and original sense of humor, and the resulting laughter is a strong component of the music of our lives.

In August, just days before our daughter was born, the buzzing of quickly descending nighthawks searching for their dinner of flies surrounded us in the woods, and afternoon thunderstorms echoed off of the nearby Lone Cone Mountain, shaking the newly carpeted floor of our cabin. Gone was the old green shag with its embedded fishing hooks that Peter had unhappily found with his bare feet.

It was into this cacophony of Nature that Ellen was born. Despite our late-night forays into medically based and disgusting names, we easily accepted the name that my mother, Faye, had come up with two years earlier when I shared that I knew we would have a daughter. Respecting her request that we consider naming our daughter after Faye's mother, "Elsie," we began to run through names that started with the letter "E." Almost immediately, my mother exclaimed, "I know—Ellen! You could name her Ellen!"

The moment she said "Ellen," I knew it to be true. Simple and light-filled, it more easily paired with the long surname of Muckerman, as opposed to a Danielle or Tabitha, a name that would have likely proved tortuously long for any child to learn how to write in kindergarten.

And now we added our own melody to the music of Nature. The sound of a newborn baby crying late into every night for many months, the sound of the diaper pail flapping shut, the sound of Ellen's coos as I held her in a shower of chittering, golden, aspen leaves that fall. In years to come, the sound of her singing the same sweat-lodge songs I had learned years earlier, her voice melding with mine and Peter's as we sang to the setting sun on summer nights.

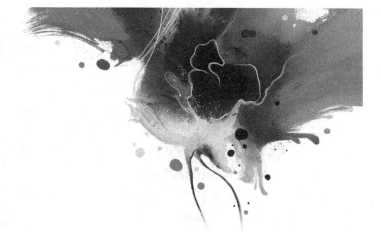

CHAPTER TWENTY-THREE

A GROWING DARKNESS

We lived in that log cabin on thirty-eight acres for a total of nine years. Aside from being sleep-deprived for the first two years of Ellen's life, I felt well in my new role as a mother. After thirty-five years of thinking only of myself, it was refreshing to focus on someone else's needs. Life became neatly organized into a series of tasks—diapers, baths, feeding, naps, stories, walks down the driveway through the woods, and moments of simply staring out the window at Lone Cone Mountain, framed by the grove of aspen trees surrounding our home.

Because our cabin was so small, and not very well-insulated, the movement of seasons through our south-facing windows seemed "larger than life." August afternoon thunderstorms shook the whole house, waking Ellen from her naps. Woodpeckers routinely jackhammered at the walls, and bats nested in our roof from May to September every year, occasionally slipping inside the house at midnight when Peter would try to whoosh them out armed with a broom and Tupperware.

The summers had gorgeous weather, allowing us to amble endlessly through the woods and invite people over for "A Midsummer Night's Dream" parties where we dressed as our favorite Shakespeare characters and dined amongst the oak trees under twinkle lights, shooting off fireworks late into the evening.

Autumns were sublime, a cascade of golden leaves showering onto the roof and driveway. One autumn day while I was teaching, Peter mistakenly dressed one-year-old Ellen in camouflage. Blending in with the wooden deck, Ellen was hard to spot, and Peter feared that she had crawled down the steps and into the woods. He had spotted mountain lion tracks a short distance away only weeks earlier. She was too young to say, "Hey Dad, I'm over here. Don't worry." When I calmly asked him how long it had taken to find her—of course, I was calm because I had returned home from school hours later and she was safely in my arms—he replied, "An eternity" (though my hunch is that she was only missing for about thirteen seconds).

Ellen grew up on the ground, in the woods, near the animals, in the elements. It was so different from my New Jersey upbringing, although I do remember picking huckleberries with my grandmother, Victoria, in the overgrown lot between our backyard and the apartment complex just across the way. In her mid-sixties, she would nimbly climb the hillside in her house dress and stockings, picking her way through the brambles.

Winters in our cabin could go one way or the other. We had some "no snow" winters, which led to drought-stricken summers with the smell of burning forest hanging in the air. One year, 30,000 acres burned for weeks only a few miles away from us. For insurance purposes, we videotaped all of our belongings in case we lost them, going from one room to the next, the western sky lit up red and flaming. Only one day later, the winds changed direction, and a twenty-minute shower—the first one of the summer—miraculously cooled off enough of the wildfire that the firemen could start to bring it under control.

Other winters brought a steady onslaught of snow—so much that we could not pass through our long, drifted driveway. The night before a big storm, I would park my car out on the road and walk back to the house. Early the next morning, Peter would drive me and Ellen about halfway down the driveway until the drifts would not allow him to go any farther. In my snowshoes, I dragged young Ellen on a sled out to the road, Peter's headlights shining weakly through the storm.

When I was feeling peaceful, the aspens swayed gently in the summer breeze, and robins sang contentedly with their fill of earthworms. The creak of the storm door, the smell of wood smoke from the fireplace, and the deer ambling past the deck at 7:30 every evening was in synchrony with my own rhythm. There was no place I'd rather be.

And when I was feeling anxious, stressed with the demands of raising a young child and working full-time, lightning strikes on the mountain threatened the drought-stricken trees, their crackles matching my unease, and the scorched grass crunched hollowly beneath my feet. Thus, I learned that we see in Nature what we feel within.

I was learning how to serve—as a wife, a mother, a teacher, and a community member—an expression of my growing spirituality with Nature as the backdrop. The routine of my life kept me from flitting off in one direction or another. No matter what I needed to discover about myself, my marriage, my family members, could not be ignored against the pristine setting of the mountains. Out in the woods, there was nothing to distract me from getting to know the darker parts of myself—the shadow. We had no television, no phone lines aside from cell phones that were outrageously expensive to use at that time, no shopping malls closer than one and a half hours away. We didn't drink or smoke—Peter had been sober for more than fifteen years at that point, and I was, thankfully, never interested—so we couldn't lose ourselves in that kind of illusion.

And still, a darkness rose in our family. I have a way of scanning for the negative, whether in my classroom—God help the kid who is quietly screwing around at the back of the band—or in my family and home life. I don't like to just leave well enough alone.

Perhaps I have high expectations of what I want my life to look and feel like. One of my closest friends once said, "You know, Rhonda—you have high expectations, but not a lot of humility," to which I laughed and exclaimed, "You're right!" Or perhaps I simply lacked trust in the process of life once I was a wife, a mother—when I had the most to lose. All of my feelings resulted in a sharpening awareness of what was happening around me, particularly in my family, and I could sense the darkness rising.

CHAPTER TWENTY-FOUR

ELIOT

E liot lived with us part-time during our years in the log cabin, from the age of ten until about fourteen when he was sent to distant boarding schools by his mother, Sharon, who had full legal custody of him. I first met Eliot in the driveway of my newly rented home in Telluride just days after meeting Peter in the shamanic meditation class. He was only six years old at that time, and we were on our way up to Dunton Hot Springs for the weekend.

Shyly hiding behind his father's leg, he peeped out to look at me, assessing this new person in his life. Unbidden but respected, my intuition piped up, "Oh, he is going to be trouble," it said of the small-for-his-size boy, blond hair falling across his forehead.

Within hours, we were happily playing and laughing amongst his toys, which covered the majority of his bedroom floor, and I heard him whisper to his Dad, "I like her—she's smart!"

Exactly how he was going to be "trouble" I didn't know, but my attention was pointed as I navigated our relationship through the years. He proved to be a disturbed boy—emotional, dramatic, and inappropriately seeking attention at school, which caused him much difficulty in forming friendships with his class-mates. I would often discover him sitting out in the elementary school hallway while I was at work, having been kicked out of one class or another. His shoulders were rounded beneath the weight of his downcast head, glasses sliding down his nose.

Eliot was extremely intelligent when it came to reading and math—off the charts, test-wise. Years later as a young man, he would act in local Shakespeare productions, memorizing pages of script as a lead actor, the difficult text rolling off his tongue. And he had his father's keen sense of humor, with the ability to mimic just about any accent. We were walking down the street one day when twelve-year-old Eliot pointed to a street sign that had fallen and was lying in the road. In a twangy, southern accent, he pointed and exclaimed, "It's a sahn; it's a sahn!"

Still, emotionally he was unstable. Who knows whether it was caused by the back-and-forth shuttling between his mom and dad, who at the time had a less-than-amicable relationship, or it was his own story as an evolving spirit. Although Eliot had two parents who loved him deeply, the bottom line was that he was insecure and isolated, talking to himself on the soccer field while his teammates ran back and forth, calling to each other throughout the game.

This state left him vulnerable to all types of addictions. He once hoarded chocolate bars at a party, hiding them in his pockets and claiming he was going to give them to friends. Pot and alcohol emerged as front-runners during his teenage and college years.

As a fourteen-year-old, he stood in our kitchen crying, "I hate myself," eyes squeezed closed and head thrown back. We held him, offering therapy and reassurances. We struggled, as all parents do, to let him know that he was loved, to support him in finding what would make him happy, and to help him find peace within himself. We worked to be the best examples we could of healthy adults, engaged in life and a spiritual path, productive and loving, but it goes without saying that no one is perfect.

Peter and I had the normal, garden-variety challenges that most couples have—stress over money, sex, parenting—which are, to me, the common things people fight over as they work toward a lifelong union with someone who is vastly different than them. When I think about marriage and raising a family, I recall the motto of the US Marines Corps commercial: "The toughest job you'll ever love."

In the earlier years of our marriage, Peter and I were hit or miss when it came to overcoming the day-to-day challenges. When we succeeded, it was like the sun shining through the woods on a blazing autumn day, but when we couldn't articulate what was happening between us, or when either of us was too stubborn to bow our heads and give in, it was like thunder rolling off the mountains, thick and cold, sending a deep chill through the drafty windows. Again, Nature is the perfect back-drop, mirroring who and where we really are.

Ellen was a constant, bright spot in our lives. She was a magical child, always singing—beautifully and on pitch—dancing in her never-ending array of tutus, and painting. She talked incessantly, only stopping the second she fell asleep. Cranky when she first awoke, she settled down as soon as she had her bottle and a family of stuffed animals around her as she laid on the kitchen floor in front of the propane heater. Her halo of tangled hair, impossible to tame into any reasonable style, made her look like a wild child.

Eliot first held her when she was four days old, fresh from the hospital on a late August afternoon. He was spellbound—not an easy accomplishment with an eleven-year-old boy—and within just a short time, as soon as Ellen had grown past what Peter calls the "cucumber phase" (the phase in which all the baby does is eat, poop, cry, and sleep), she was equally captivated by Eliot. They held hands in the back seat of the car, staring adoringly into each other's eyes. I believe they were reencountering each other after many lifetimes, a prince and his princess. All was right with the world when they were together, though it didn't happen often enough for Ellen. On the one or two days a week Eliot was in our home, she would run through the house, gleefully calling, "Eliot! Eliot!" when he came through the door, loaded down with his school backpack, dejected by another day out in the world.

Still, the seasons changed from one to the next, and after nine years of work, love, laughter, and winters with eight-feet-tall Christmas trees and too many snow-drifted driveways, we left our log cabin in the woods for a new house in town where we could more easily access school and work. Peter and I had been married for thirteen years at that point; Ellen was eight and Eliot was a nineteen-year-old college student we only saw occasionally on breaks from his New England liberal arts school.

We had had our time in Nature, and it was time to move back into the material world out of respect for Ellen's education and accessibility to friends, along with a greater ease for me in managing my work life and home responsibilities. A new, well-insulated home, with a gas fireplace, gourmet kitchen, and music room awaited us. From its south-facing windows, we could barely see the tip of Lone Cone Mountain rising over the distant ridge, and that was just fine with me.

CHAPTER TWENTY-FIVE

NORWOOD

We moved in the spring of 2008, the wind gusting constantly, my clothes flapping around me and grit in my eyes as I carried in one box after another. The house was "prefab," constructed in a factory in Missouri before being transported across plains and mountains. My middle school band members and I watched it arrive on a cold, February afternoon, lifted by a crane, one half at a time, onto its foundation.

In addition to the convenience of living in town, I was hoping the move would offer a cure, or at least a distraction, from the darker, still unarticulated issues that had begun to emerge during our years in the log cabin. Having enjoyed lush forest and mountain views for the past nine years, we now looked out on a barren street with only a few, newly planted cottonwood trees. The wind howled every day that spring, punctuated only by the barking of neighborhood dogs. Within six months of our move, the value of our new house, and of the log cabin we were still trying to sell, plummeted when the real estate bubble burst, leaving us with two house payments each month and an undercurrent of financial stress between me and Peter.

The reality was that Peter hadn't really wanted to move into town. He loved his morning commute from the log cabin to his trailer just down the driveway, coffee cup in hand. I was the one who pushed for the new house in town, even though we had not yet sold the log cabin. I was captivated by the drop-in bathtub with whirlpool jets and the idea of having next-door neighbors after years of living in isolation, our nearest neighbors several miles away.

Amidst our daily routine of work and school, a chasm was slowly developing between me and Peter. We were, at that time, fundamentally different people—I the eternal optimist, the cheerleader, waving the banner of God and new beginnings and he the cynic who felt pushed into building a home that he didn't really want. His addictive nature was a source of stress for me as well, whether that meant too much coffee, sugar, or negative thinking. There were many days our new house was filled with a dark cloud, and I distanced myself from him through judgment, occupying myself in the business of being a teacher and a mother.

Fourteen years earlier when we were dating, we laid side by side as I bared my heart to him, stressing about something in my thirty-year-old existence. He nodded, reached over and wiped a tear from my cheek, then pulled the blanket over my shoulder. I naively assumed that Peter "got me," that he understood what made me tick, and that he was in complete agreement with my cosmology, my beliefs. We became quickly and intimately involved, swept along on a current of chemistry that did not allow for either one of us to really get to know the other person. In a blush of hormones, pheromones, and attraction, we so easily saw the positive attributes in each other. Peter's daily habit of drinking lots of coffee presented as quirky rather than an indicator of an addictive personality, and my propensity toward anxiety and worry hadn't yet fully bloomed into a need to control everything coming down the pike.

If our early relationship had been a course of study, "Peter and Rhonda 101," we would have been relegated to taking a remedial class before marrying to make up for our lost foundation of pure friendship that the best marriages have. The syllabus would have included such topics as: "Basic Philosophies of Life—Cynic or Optimist?" and "Power and Control in Marriage: Does it Really Matter How She Cuts the Red Bell Peppers?"

Since this class did not exist, we spent many years uncovering the sources of our friction, naming them one by one: addiction, anxiety, depression, judgment. To our credit, we stayed in the room, sometimes for many hours, dissecting where these shadows came from. We explained our perspectives, our sides, ad nauseum until I could stand it no longer, drawing a line with my toe one night in the imaginary sand on our bathroom floor right next to the drop-in bathtub with the whirlpool jets. We went to our separate corners for a time, but thankfully still stood united in the day-to-day tasks of making money to pay two house payments a month, trying to grow tomatoes in the barren soil of Norwood, and raising Ellen.

Thankfully, Peter's sense of humor would shine through once in a while, lifting us and reminding me that we were still in the right setting and circumstances to evolve. Lessons of patience, humility, and service kept us together even through the times of doubt and frustration.

As Peter is twenty years older than me, he experienced some difficulties with his health when we lived in Norwood. A partial knee replacement with its long and painful recovery period tested the limits of my patience as I worked to maintain the household, take care of Ellen, and be his nurse. Groaning loudly each time Peter rang the bell from his place in bed, I failed the test but learned valuable information about myself: I am a terrible nurse and am much better suited toward tasks like reconciling our bank statements.

Peter's knee surgery was a mere warm-up for his encounters with not one, not two, but three brown recluse spiders. Those scientifically astute readers might interject at this point and say, "Wait—there are no brown recluse spiders in the mountains of Colorado!" But you must understand that our new, prefab home had been constructed in Missouri, where these poisonous arachnids thrive. When our home was transported on its flatbed semi, a family of brown recluses was already in residence. One year later, Peter was bitten several times while working in the crawl space, noting their super size and speed. They were large bites, the fangs clearly demarked. Weeks later, his hand shook uncontrollably when he reached for his coffee cup on the kitchen island. In the ensuing months, I found that I had to repeat myself often in conversation, as Peter was unable to track on what I was saying. At the dinner table he withdrew from our conversations while Ellen babbled on about her day.

After experiencing a series of symptoms ranging from tremors to brain fog, he was diagnosed by our naturopath as suffering from brown recluse toxins. He embarked on a detoxification program involving the use of essential oils, which caused his hands to erupt in inflamed blisters for many months, and out of necessity, I stepped into the role of caregiver once again.

This I did not do gracefully.

I already felt as if I carried the bulk of responsibility in our family as a regular wage-earner, mother, cook, and housekeeper, not to mention the underlying—and at times overwhelming—role of cheerleader to my pessimistic partner. Now I was required to step up further. I did what I could to bow my head and rise up in service, but there were plenty of times when I snapped impatiently at Peter or Ellen, the strain clear in my eyes and heart.

Adding to our collective strain as a family was the reality that Eliot was expressing more and more of his addictive qualities. Now in his early twenties, his use of alcohol became extreme. The rare times that Eliot came to visit, he smelled of alcohol and was unable to spend the night since we did not have booze, nor did we allow its use, in our home. When he left after dinner to return to his home in Telluride, Ellen would walk slowly to her room, head downcast, on to her next art project or song, a princess whose prince was riding off to an unknown kingdom for reasons she could not yet understand.

And for me, the intuition I received the moment I met Eliot seventeen years earlier was realized.

In a quiet moment, we told him on our living room couch what we believed to be true—that he was headed for either prison or death. We did what we could to guide him toward a path that included God, sobriety, forgiveness, and hope. Eliot just shook his head, his eyes darkened, arrogance blooming.

CHAPTER TWENTY-SIX

SAN MIGUEL

B y the time Ellen was three years old, I had begun teaching in the small, rural school district nearby. I wanted to be part of the school that Ellen would eventually attend. This little town, not unlike the town of Vassar where I landed my first job thirteen years earlier, had one gas station, one grocery story, one saloon/restaurant, and a number of churches and liquor stores. It had a rich ranching history, though unless you and the previous three generations of your family had been born and raised there, you were definitely an outsider. Still, we liked the simplicity of small-town life and felt it would be the best place to raise Ellen.

With such a lean school district—only one class of students per grade—I was responsible for the entire music program, K–12. My schedule consisted of general music for kindergarten through fifth grade and band for fifth grade through high school, as well as an after-school choir for middle and high school students. All in all, the kids were sweet and ready to learn, arriving at my room in a single-file, almost military line, with even the toughest kids silent. Because they were so well-mannered, I managed to cover about 30 percent more material in any given class than I ever had before. My new students sailed through sight-singing and rhythmic exercises in kindergarten through third grade and recorders in fourth grade to become some of the best middle school band students I ever had.

For seven years, I arrived at school every day at 7:30 a.m. The smell of freshly waxed floors accompanied me to my classroom, which was an abandoned, windowless, all-purpose room of sorts that I divided into a general music space for my younger students and a band rehearsal area for my middle and high school students. I straightened the chairs before each rehearsal, placing folders and pencils neatly on each stand, creating an orderly space in which we could rise to the music I had selected.

I greeted each student by name as they entered the room, working to establish a connection, a community, a family. Over the years, some of my students would smile warmly and share some news with me about their days, their families, their accomplishments. But more often than not, the band members would file in dutifully, give a faint nod, get their instruments, and silently sit behind their stands until I stood on the podium to begin rehearsal. As we warmed up our instruments and began to rehearse, the students gradually awakened as layers of sound encircled us, the percussionists hunched over their triangles, snares, and glockenspiel, brass players hurriedly emptying their spit valves so as not to miss their next entrance. These kids could play! They had no idea that what they were doing was hard.

Day after day, we made magic. And day after day, I released my students back into the hallway where their peers awaited them and said things like, "Ewwww—you're in band?"

My band members would hang their heads, eyes downcast, and shrug their shoulders, mute. Had they forgotten what we just accomplished? I wondered why they didn't straighten up and say, "Yeah, I'm in band. It's great, you should hear us!"

But just like our tomatoes that wouldn't grow in the barren soil, the music program couldn't take root. Demoralized, I wondered how I would continue to teach there, having always imagined that I would stay until Ellen graduated, which was still eight years in the future; I had already been in the district for seven years at that point.

That same summer I registered Ellen for a music camp in Telluride called Rock and Roll Academy. Housed in a small private school on the outskirts of Telluride, the Rock and Roll Academy is not unlike the movie *School of Rock*. Kids come in, pick up an instrument that they have never played before, pick out a song—"Smoke on the Water" is a popular one—and learn only what they need to in order to perform. No note-reading, no flashcards, no scales—so different from my classical training. Ellen spent two hours each afternoon that week in the red studio with three other kids, rotating from one instrument to another, the freedom and exhilaration of playing in a band awakening a dream of her own within. After her first day she met me in the lobby of the school and exclaimed, "My life is in that room!"

Each afternoon that week, I waited for Ellen in the lobby, looking at the student artwork that adorned the walls, the sounds of rock and roll filtering down the hallway. On the second day, I sat on a bench in the lobby, my butt sore from too much driving and waiting, and I allowed my mind to float off and closed my eyes.

A luminous cloud approached from my left peripheral vision. Because I knew what it was, and because I did not want to face the upheaval that would happen as a result of letting this thought in, I turned my head to the right, willfully ignoring what it had to tell me. After a moment, I knew I could not pretend that I had not sensed this intuition coming. I opened my eyes and received it. Ellen would attend this Mountain School where Rock and Roll Academy was held. Her artwork would adorn the walls and her music would filter down its hallway.

We were moving back to Telluride.

Peter and I talked late into that night, a full moon illuminating our new future. I reasoned, "If Ellen is going to attend the Mountain School, I no longer want to teach in Norwood. I wonder what I could do in Telluride."

Since I had already signed a contract for the upcoming year in Norwood, we agreed that we would take time to figure things out. Ellen would be in fourth grade and still needed to apply to the Mountain School, and I wanted to finish my eighth year well.

Later that month, I had a dream. I was standing next to John Yankee, the Telluride Choral Society director from my early days in Telluride, in front of a large ensemble, both of us conducting simultaneously, synchronized. A moment later, he stopped conducting, turned, and exited the stage, leaving me with the sole responsibility of leadership of the ensemble. I could feel the new weight settling on my shoulders, pushing them downward, but I continued moving my arms, and the band kept playing.

A few weeks later, on the fifteenth anniversary of the week I moved to Telluride, a friend and fellow musician from my early years in Telluride called and invited me to lunch to discuss something "personal." Not having seen Deb in quite a while, I couldn't imagine what she wanted to discuss, but I happily agreed since I was going to be in town that day anyway. As we caught up over burgers and fries, I kept waiting for the "personal" part of our conversation, but Deb was telling me about the Telluride Choral Society, its financial difficulties in the midst of the recession, and how its current director was making plans to move on to other professional opportunities. I kept thinking, "Why is she telling me all of this?"

Finally, Deb said, "Rhonda, I know that you are really happy with your life in Norwood and all, but is there any way you would consider being our next director?"

In that moment, my recent dream fully revealed itself. I was about to step into a new musical responsibility, and the luminous intuition that we would be moving back to Telluride made sense.

I didn't even take the time to inhale before I blurted out, "Yes!" going on to confess that I was not all that happy in Norwood at this point. I explained, "We were actually planning on Ellen going to school in Telluride next year, and I was wondering what I was going to do. So, yes—yes, I would definitely consider being the next director!"

Deb nodded, her eyes brightening as she leaned back in her chair. We began to discuss the details—when I might be able to start rehearsals, which groups (from children to adults) were already formed—until we reached a logical stopping point for the time being. We made plans to connect again soon after she had spoken with the other board members, hugged, and said our goodbyes.

I walked across town, weaving my way through the crowded farmers' market, and sat on a rock on the bank of the San Miguel river, the autumn sunshine warm on my face and shoulders. The water tumbled over the rocks serenely, a slow pace compared to its rushing tempo just a month earlier when August monsoons caused the river to swell right up to the trail. I gazed at the golden aspens covering the hillside, then bowed my head in thanks, a new song filling my heart.

CHAPTER TWENTY-SEVEN

ILLNESS AND DEATH

T he view from the north-facing windows in our new condo was dominated by the San Sophia ridge, snow-capped and imposing. The direction of the North in native cultures can signify the attainment of Wisdom, the completion of a cycle around the Medicine Wheel. As I stood in our 800-square-foot home, even on this brilliant day just after the summer solstice, I could not ignore the darkness I felt was ahead for our family. The mountains kept us in our place, saying, "This is reality. There is no running from it."

Ellen and I had commuted almost daily for three years from Norwood to Telluride, deep in the canyon along the San Miguel river, most mornings too early to see the sun rise. While she attended the Mountain School, I prepared for my rehearsals with the Telluride Choral Society, taking up residence in the public library, a whole table to myself to study scores and send emails to my singers from my pink laptop.

After my late-afternoon choir rehearsals, we returned to Norwood through the darkening canyon once again, though we would get a brief glimpse of the sun just before it set when we got to Wright's Mesa. Evenings were filled with dinner, home-work, and bedtime, the same cycle repeating every weekday.

The pull toward Telluride was palpable, not only for the con-venience of avoiding ninety minutes in the car each day—though I treasured the time Ellen and I had to discuss all manner of things—but also for the warmth of renewed friendships in the music and school communities. Although our family had been away for fif-teen years, we were greeted on the streets as if we had never left with hugs and lengthy conversations on sun-warmed benches.

Our move was accelerated by the sudden death of Eliot's mother, Sharon. Hiking alone while on vacation in Mexico, she died of a heart attack at the age of fifty-seven, leaving her son with a gut full of unresolved emotions. He landed in the hospital several months later with a perforated intestine, and we knew that we needed to be closer to Eliot, hoping to provide a more secure foundation, a new beginning, an alternative to his loneli-ness and ever-increasing use of alcohol.

Only steps away from our building, there is a trail through the woods that leads to the Galloping Goose trail, which was formerly where the narrow-gauge railway of the same name trav-eled along the San Miguel River, down to Ilium Valley and up toward Lizard Head pass. Its proximity to our home was one of the greatest saving graces of my day-to-day life. Down the hill, past the school, and along the river it wound. Across the foot-bridge, I could anoint myself in the icy waters of Skunk Creek, and into the woods, I was free to link with my Creator, the scent of spruce and aspen sharp, my eyes bathed in green and gold.

Shortly after we moved, Peter and I set out to explore the trail. As we headed down the hillside, Peter in front, I noticed a peculiar movement of his left arm for the first time. With each step he took, his forearm flagged out behind him, waving uncontrollably several times per second. At first, we laughed at this anomaly, which we thought was surely some mechanical issue as a result of lifting too many boxes and furniture during the move.

Peter had always been virile—a chopper of firewood, standing for days on end while teaching wilderness medical classes. He was the guy you wanted to have around if you or someone you loved got hurt, carefully administering bandages and splints and flushing out wounds. Aside from a partial knee replacement, a couple of minor surgeries (hernia and gallbladder), and his run-ins with the brown recluse spiders three years earlier, Peter was in good health, easily looking ten years younger than he really was.

Still, his occasional flagging left arm and some weeks later the minute, "pill-rolling" motion in his left thumb that surfaced one evening while we were watching television were signs of something that neither one of us wanted to acknowledge out loud. Without daring to say what we suspected might be happening, I began downloading books on my Kindle that would explain the strange symptoms Peter had developed.

You might wonder at this point, "Why didn't you want to say the words?" To this question, I offer my growing understanding that words have the power to direct the course of our lives. I am a student and practitioner of an ancient healing art called "Jin Shin Jyutsu," having been first introduced to it after suffering through a case of the chicken pox at the age of thirty-four, which I caught from Eliot. After one treatment, I felt like a million bucks, the sun shining through me in a way it hadn't in years. Captivated, I began to study, and in the years that followed, I adopted the Jin Shin philosophy that what we call diseases and illnesses—the "scary labels"—are better thought of as health "projects" that can have creative outcomes and possibilities. While the words "Parkinson's disease" did not cross our lips for some time, the mountains to the north of our home provided an image of a challenge that would be almost insurmountable, requiring superhuman effort against all odds.

Late into the night, I read anything that would offer hope—books that spoke of magnesium deficiencies, iodine deficiencies, baking soda and amino acid cures, healing the emotions and body through tapping, meditations and affirmations, high-protein diets, high-fat diets, no-carb diets, plant-based diets, hypnosis and surrender, visualization, positive thinking, quantum physics, mind over matter, homeopathy, ortho-bionomy, and water-based medicine, just to name a few. And early each day I rose to conduct my beginning and middle school band students—I had returned to the Telluride school district on a part-time basis—and my children and adult choirs into the evenings.

My cell phone rang one sunny, March afternoon as I drove up the final hill near my home. There was going to be a big dress rehearsal that evening with my adult choirs, as our annual spring concert was in two days.

Recognizing my husband's number on the screen, I said, "Hi honey," as I answered the phone. What followed was unintelligible, a torrent of syllables in a voice I didn't recognize.

"He's dead; Eliot's dead!"

"Who is this?" I yelled, my chest constricted, my head shaking "no" even before I understood.

"It's Peter, Rhonda—it's Peter!"

And with the force of my husband's words, in a voice so anguished that it didn't resemble his confident bass, we were initiated into a moment that no one ever imagines they will be in. Peter, Ellen, and I were tapped on the shoulder, removed from our usual lives, and placed into an empty room where even the most sincere condolences and casseroles could not gain entrance.

The mountains to the north bore witness as later that evening, at Ellen's request, the three of us made our way down the still snowy hillside to the banks of the San Miguel river. We stood dazed while Ellen, a princess without her prince, picked up a stone, held it to her heart, and placed it in her pocket. Together we climbed the trail, our feet sodden and cold, both of Peter's arms now flagging behind him.

CHAPTER TWENTY-EIGHT

DROWNING

One year after Eliot's death, a friend of mine asked, "If this past year were a chapter in your book, what would you name the chapter?"

I responded quickly, "Rhonda goes to hell and back."

But that answer doesn't tell you much about the year—and years—after Eliot passed. That answer reveals more about my nature. Two people in my life have called me "dramatic," to which at first, I recoiled, thinking, "No, that's not who I am." But more recently I have allowed myself to feel the possibility that I might be just that, at least in circumstances when I am pushed to my limits.

I was born under the sign of Leo. Actually, I am a "double Leo," since my ascendant sign is within Leo as well, which gives me the capacity for a big, forceful personality if I so choose. This is of great assistance in my line of work. I am completely at home conducting large groups of musicians in front of larger audiences.

As was once explained to me by a reputable astrologer in Seattle (And by reputable, I mean not the kind of astrologer who claims to predict one's future), "Aaaah, your future husband's name will start with the letter 'D,' or, er, perhaps the letter 'S.'"

Reputable, as in clarifying the influences at work in my life, given the position of the planets when I was born.

He explained that, in addition to my double Leo nature, my moon was in Scorpio, "Your emotions are kind of like nuclear waste in the depths of the earth," he said, his arm stretching downward, grasping and twisting my inner muck and bringing it upward to my double-Leo, sunny personality.

I watched, enthralled—yes, that was me! A squaring off between the dark and light, nuclear waste and brilliant sunshine, despair and optimism. With these two essential aspects of my nature, I entered the most difficult chapter of my life.

The empty room in which we lived consisted of only a few essential questions: "How did this happen? Could we have done more? How will we go on?"

The first question was answered within moments of finding him. The detritus of empty Dust-Off cans were strewn around where he had overdosed on his living room couch. Unbeknownst to his family and friends, he ordered cases of it online and stored them upstairs in his house where no one would see them. In an attempt to stop drinking alcohol, Eliot had developed a habit of huffing the chemical substance—difluoroethane—that is used to clear the dust from a computer keyboard.

The second question, I believe, torments every parent who has lost a child into a day-by-day, year-by-year reckoning of every conversation, every mistake, every flaw. I accompanied Peter as he began to make his way through the labyrinth of memories and emotions that made up the almost twenty-six years of Eliot's life, questioning himself at every turn.

At times he would shake his head and say, "I could have been more present with him," to which I would respond with one example after another of how present Peter really was. "Remember all those weekends you spent together up at Dunton? Remember how you talked every morning at breakfast before Eliot went to school and how we worked with him at dinner every night? How you took him camping and shooting, made fireworks together?"

The examples were endless. Peter had truly been a doting father, listening to every word Eliot said. And although Eliot communicated less as he got older, especially as his addictions deepened, Peter continued to try to break through, offering to go to AA meetings with Eliot. The last time Peter saw him alive, he brought some soup to help with Eliot's stomach flu. They spoke for some time, Peter questioning Eliot about whether he was ready to get sober.

"How're you doing with that first step?" Peter asked, referring to the first of twelve steps that make up the AA program: "We admitted we were powerless over alcohol and that our lives had become unmanageable."

"Not there yet," Eliot answered briefly.

Later, as Peter got up to leave, Eliot called out his final words from the couch, "I love you. You're a good dad."

This was the greatest gift that Eliot gave Peter, a balm that we could apply every time the question arose.

As to the third question of how we would go on, we lived through our days as we always had—work, school, spiritual life, grocery shopping, ballet recitals—but there was now a cloud, hanging over everything, the darkness that I had anticipated before moving back to Telluride fully revealed. When I tried to imagine what our lives would be like in a year, or two, or five, all I saw was darkness, an endless ceiling extending from one horizon to the other, way beyond the mountains to the north.

In addition, Peter's symptoms were worsening month after month. The slight pill-rolling motion in his left hand had spread to his right with a greater amplitude that became more and more noticeable. He lost strength in his legs and his face became "masked," showing only an expression of numbness and grief. Since he was in his early seventies, I encouraged him to retire from teaching to reduce his stress and concentrate more on rehabilitation and healing.

After retiring, Peter filled his days with an endless regimen of qi gong, meditation, and physical therapy, alternated with time spent reading in his chair in an attempt to regain some energy. He tried every natural remedy we could find, including amino acids, CoQ10, fish oils, vitamins, velvet bean extract, homeopathy, CBD and hemp oils, and mushroom extracts. Twice a day, Peter brought down an arm-length tray of supplements from the top of our refrigerator and swallowed them dutifully, eyes blankly staring ahead.

Several times over the course of a two years, he tried Western medicine's answer to Parkinson's disease, "Sinemet"—a synthesized form of dopamine that relieves some of the symptoms but can also cause numerous side effects and can be toxic if used long-term—but after only a few doses, he was shaking worse than ever and could only lie incapacitated in bed. Leary, we turned away from pharmaceuticals and worked to find the root cause of the illness.

Could it have been caused by some hidden emotional trauma from childhood, or did Peter's addictive personality (even though he was no longer addicted to anything) play a part in the depletion of dopamine that causes Parkinson's? Trying one theory after another, we experimented with Jin Shin Jyutsu, acupuncture, the "tapping" technique—sometimes hopeful that we had found the root cause, other times despairing when a reduction in symptoms turned out to be only temporary.

I, in turn, took on more responsibility supporting our family both materially and emotionally, holding together the daily routine of our lives and providing reassurance, optimism, and clarity when needed. For the first year or so after Eliot died, I survived each day, ready to serve in whatever way was needed, being present with my family, then going to school to teach middle schoolers, rehearsing my choirs after school, picking up groceries on the way home, paying bills, making dinner, then finishing out the night by supporting Ellen and Peter as I could. Some nights were easy, hanging out and watching a movie while eating spaghetti, but others were filled with grief and tears and anguish, and I would rise to their needs, setting aside my own need for rest and rejuvenation.

Sometime during the year after Eliot's death, I realized that the shock and upheaval we had experienced in its wake had been replaced by the constant wearing down of living with the reality of a chronic and progressive illness. From the moment we awoke every morning, it was there, demanding a response.

This is when I learned I am a fighter. My husband might have an awful disease, but I would not accept that there was no cure for it. I believed that if we kept looking, kept faithful, that something would come along to bring healing. And so, for two years, I continued to carry the torch, reminding Peter to use his words well, eat well, think well. It was, frankly, exhausting. Feeling trapped by my circumstances, I began to see the nuclear waste within me that my astrologer had spoken of—despair, anger, hatred. Each time I pushed it back down, changed the channel. Each time the light in my eyes grew dimmer, my face hardening.

CHAPTER TWENTY-NINE

MACHU PICCHU

D ay by day, we continued to function. We served our community as best we could, and we sometimes laughed or celebrated, a momentary respite from the shuffling march toward an unknown horizon. Her grief placing her in unfamiliar territory, Ellen ventured into the world of the American teenager, the light in her eyes diminishing, sleeping past noon in the cave of her room after I waited up for her late on Saturday nights.

Working to pick ourselves up, we planned a trip to Peru in the summer of 2016. Peter and I had wanted to visit Machu Picchu almost twenty years earlier, but we had held off. I knew it would be important to make the trip with our daughter, but she hadn't been born yet. With Ellen almost seventeen years old and Peter still able to somewhat tolerate the rigors of international travel, we took advantage of a slim window during our summer break.

Before I go on, I have to pause for a moment to share one of my most deeply held beliefs. From the age of ten, when I secretly read a novel called *The Reincarnation of Peter Proud* (much to the anger of my mother who was not happy at my delving into a trashy adult novel), I have felt completely comfortable with the concept of reincarnation. Indeed, it was—and still is—the only way I can make sense of deep connections I feel when meeting and recognizing people or places for the "first" time. I know to my core that the main characters in my story, as well as the talents that I possess, are part of a continuing line through lifetimes as I evolve.

And so, I found myself on a bus crowded to the gills with other tourists in the early morning hours, scaling the mountainside, switchback by dangerous switchback, ascending to Machu Picchu. I was separated from Peter and Ellen; they had been allowed to catch a bus some time earlier due to Peter's inability to stand in the 2,000-person queue that had formed by 4:00 a.m. Ellen was allowed to accompany him at the head of the line, and we had agreed to meet at the entrance of Machu Picchu once I arrived.

I stood in line alone, shivering in the pre-dawn light with strangers who I sensed were hostile after our tour guide snuck me ahead of hundreds of other tourists who had been waiting for hours to catch a bus. Not moving, I tried to take up as little space as possible, avoiding eye contact and sorely missing the warmth of my family.

Finally on the bus, I had a window seat from which I could see the oncoming returning busses speeding down the switchbacks, pushing our bus to the edge of the road. "I might actually die on this road without my family," I thought to myself.

The thought was perhaps a bit dramatic, but I was already feeling emotional. I was ignoring the road as best as I could, looking at the jungle that carpeted the mountainside, when I felt the awareness that I had lived here before welling up inside me. The thought bloomed within me—it had taken many lifetimes for me and Peter and Ellen to be reunited in this place, coming full circle.

This wasn't just a thought that happened to cross my mind as the other tourists were chatting loudly around me, exchanging Clif bars and water bottles. The truth erupted from me in a series of snotty sobs, urging me to hide my face in the window, my one tissue wet and shredded in my hand. I bowed my head, closing my eyes. The sunlight finally extended into the valley, into my heart, verifying my realization, and it warmed me as I, with reddened and puffy eyes, exited the bus, scanning the crowds for my family.

Finally reunited, we embraced, and they nodded in recognition as I shared my vision; they were used to my intuitions and dreams, knowing the extent to which they had guided our life. We explored the ruins together, each step illuminated by the sun and by the words of our tour guide, who patiently waited while we took break after break to allow Peter to rest along the way.

On our last night in Cusco, we spent time with a man named José, a friend of a friend in our spiritual community. He owned a local tour guide company and later told us that when he heard my voice on the telephone, he thought, "I must meet these people," and ventured out to our hotel downtown.

José had a talent for "reading" people's lives, both past and present, in the pattern of coca leaves spilled from a teacup. It reminded me of my time with Marguerite twenty-six years earlier. The four of us sat close together on the two beds in our tiny hotel room while he shared glimmers of our past together in Peru. I had worked with textiles and architecture and healing, and Peter had been a warrior who had died young. Everything José said made sense; it was consistent with who we knew ourselves to be. As a teenager I had been drawn to architecture for a brief time, and as an adult, I was always reading one book after another about alternative forms of healing. Peter had been in the Marine Corps as a young man, so it rang true that he had a history of being a warrior.

Whether José's musings were accurate or not, we enjoyed the moment, allowing ourselves to be fully present with the scent of coca leaves and the possibility that a door to the future might crack open just wide enough for us to gain some hope or guidance in the face of Peter's deteriorating health.

The room quieted, and I could feel Peter gathering his thoughts and courage. "Will my health get better, enough to be able to serve in my community?" he asked quietly, hands trembling in his lap.

José tossed the leaves again and again, staring into the patterns, his head tilted to one side, listening. I looked down at my lap, concentrating on playing with a loose strand on my sweater as the sounds from the courtyard below filtered up into our room. I didn't want to rush him.

"Ele vai melhorar," he finally said, "mas não completamente."

"You're going to get better," I translated the Portuguese, "but not completely."

Peter nodded his understanding, and we tried on for size the first words of hope that anyone had ever said to us regarding his illness. Scanning the bare walls in silence, I linked with my intuition, and a clear voice in my head resounded, "José is an instrument of Me."

It was the same voice I heard on that rainy April night in Seattle when I asked God, "Where is my spiritual family?" and it responded, "Go to Telluride."

After twenty-two years, I had come to trust that voice, its orientations forming a firm foundation with me. I inhaled and allowed the words to take root, the possibility of a new future on the horizon.

Late that night I had a dream as I lied sleeping next to Peter in the small bed of our hotel room, Ellen across from us in her twin bed. In the dream, we had left our hotel door overlooking the courtyard wide open, and we were vulnerable to outside, negative influences. I was paralyzed and could do nothing when an agitated, native man entered our tiny room, paced to the back, then turned around, crossed the room once again, and exited, slamming the door behind him.

The next morning, Ellen confirmed that she too had felt a negative force within our room during the night, and with the coming of dawn, felt it dissipate into the air. We left Peru that day, complete, its light with us as we returned home to the snow-capped mountains of Colorado.

CHAPTER THIRTY

ROAD TRIP

The wheels of Ellen's Toyota Sequoia, a.k.a. James, thrummed along Interstate 40 as we entered Memphis, Paul Simon's "Graceland" pounding through the speakers as we bounced our heads, singing along. Elvis's homestead, a slice of Americana not to be missed, marked the final hours of our three-day, 1,500-mile journey to settle Ellen in at Belmont University in Nashville, TN.

Our travels had started a week earlier, 300 miles west of Telluride in Salt Lake City, UT. After packing all of Ellen's belongings and stacking the boxes in her ten-by-ten room, we raced westward in the opposite direction to see, for the second time,

Ellen's idol, Jack White. Six hours of driving, followed by two hours of standing in line for general admission seating, was the prelude to screaming at the top of our lungs as the bass reverberated straight through us while we sweated in our blue jeans and ninety-five-degree weather. I pretended I had the energy and stamina of a teenager as we all stood shoulder to shoulder. Jack White dominated the stage, his puppy-dog haircut flopping over his ears. He was a humble performer, eyes glistening as he thanked us for coming out.

Geographically, it was an illogical hop to the west, this impromptu trip just days before the big journey of escorting Ellen to Nashville for her professional downbeat, which was taking place exactly thirty-six years after my own downbeat at MSU. But musically and spiritually, the trip was perfect. Ellen had decided to pursue her own dream of entering the music industry as a talented singer/songwriter, a manifestation of my friend's dream nineteen years earlier in which Ellen was singing from my pregnant belly.

So with the force of Jack White's music still rocking within us, we packed her silver Sequoia with her guitars and amplifiers, clothing and toiletries—Who needs to see out the rearview mirror?—and crossed through new landscape together. We wound our way down through New Mexico, sometimes exiting the interstate for a brief hop and a Coke on historic Route 66, singing smoothly about getting our kicks. Wind generators waved at us as we passed through the panhandle of Texas while we twanged out the lyrics of "Amarillo Sky," and the steamy, sultry climate of Oklahoma and Arkansas sang its own song to us of frogs and crickets chirping while we shaded ourselves underneath an old weeping willow tree just off a dusty county road.

This was to be my last time with Ellen for at least a couple of months, and my heart was bursting at the fullness of delivering her into a new chapter of her life. I drank in every moment of those 1,500 miles, including our tour of Graceland as we streamed through the sixties opulence, posing for the required photo, our faces glistening in the August humidity.

I wondered what this next chapter would hold for me and Peter as we entered into the life of "empty nesters." Two years had passed since our trip to Peru, and the shine of José's prediction that Peter's health would improve had worn off. Despite an infusion of 187 million stem cells several months earlier, Peter's symptoms had been worsening—albeit gradually—though we still held out hope that necessary repair work was happening at an imperceptible level and would continue throughout what we were told could be a year-long process.

When one is dealing with a chronic illness and all of its attendant caretaking requirements, it can be a respite of sorts to focus on the "normal" activities of daily life. In my case, I immersed myself in getting Ellen ready for the move to college. I spent much of the summer arranging the necessary details— dental appointments, doctor's appointments, tuition payments, shopping for her dorm room, planning our trip to Nashville. It was a welcome distraction, but there came a time when every item on my list was checked off.

On Sunday, August 19, just two days after Ellen's nineteenth birthday, we left her after a tearful embrace on campus, surrounded by hundreds of other parents doing exactly the same thing. The door on our active, child-rearing days had firmly closed, and the reality that it would be just me and Peter, along with our attendant challenges, had arrived, returning us to the mountains of Colorado.

We sat down on the cement steps in front of the Chick-fil-A on campus, and I sobbed. My daughter—and my heart—were only a few hundred yards away, only separated from us by some buildings and a campus full of magnolia trees. Yet, my horizon, bleak and heavy, looked and felt completely different from what I imagined hers looked like. In my loss and anger and fear, I exploded at Peter, shaking my head, woefully imagining what it would be like when we resumed our lives in Colorado. He sat next to me, still and constant, and when the storm moved on, we stood up and left campus, an empty distance stretching between us.

CHAPTER THIRTY-ONE

MYSTIC RIVER

P eter and I had decided that before returning home from Nashville, we would take a little vacation—just a few days in Mystic, CT, plus a short stop in New Jersey to visit my mother. My father had passed away two years earlier and now, after fifty-four years of marriage, my mother was bravely making her way out into the world, filling her days with Friends of the Library meetings and volunteer work. It wasn't an easy time for her, so a visit to the "nest" just before her seventy-seventh birthday seemed appropriate.

While Peter and I stayed at the Whaler's Inn in Mystic, I had a dream. We were in our kitchen (though it's funny that our "dream" homes never look like our real homes). This kitchen had an island in the center, which was built solidly with mortared, glass blocks. We were in the midst of a remodel, and we realized that the only way to open up the space between us was to demolish the island, swinging sledgehammers over our heads, smashing it, blocks shattering at our feet.

A moment later, Ellen and I stood in the front room of the house and assessed the old furniture, which was taking up every last cubic inch of space. We smiled at each other as we envisioned how we would get rid of it all, turning the front room into a music rehearsal space, complete with piano and bookshelves.

I shared this dream with Peter later that day as we sat on a bench on the Mystic River; he needed to rest frequently, usually every block or so, when we walked. The church bells were chiming the tune to "O Sanctissima," the same hymn I had sung over twenty years earlier in those first rehearsals of the Telluride Choral Society, saving all of us "in peril on the sea."

As the strains floated over the town of Mystic, my brow finally unfurrowed as I exhaled the stress I had been carrying since leaving Ellen in Nashville. The scent of the river, heavy and damp, massaged my heart and lifted from it the sorrow that had taken up residence since our family began drowning four years earlier, the moment Eliot had died.

With only a few words, I forgave Peter for all of the challenges—real or imagined—that his illness had presented. I forgave myself for not living up to the perhaps impossible standards I had imposed upon myself. I forgave Life for not turning out the way I had hoped it would.

And so the glass block island was destroyed, not with a sledgehammer, but with forgiveness and its ensuing peace. Overhead, the seagulls danced, lifted by a fresh breeze.

CHAPTER THIRTY-TWO

COZUMEL

T he harmonies of Monteverdi's "Ecco Mormorar
L'Onde" swirl throughout the front room of our tiny
condo. Five of us sway and dip toward each other as we
work the sixteenth-century Italian lyrics:

> "Here, now, the waves murmur and the leaves and young
> poplars tremble in the morning breeze.
> And upon the green branches the enchanting birds sing
> sweetly.
> And the East smiles.

Here, now, the dawn breaks and is mirrored in the sea,
and calms the sky,
and adorns the light frost with pearls, and gilds the tow-
ering mountains.
Oh lovely, gentle dawn.
The breeze is your messenger, and you are the breeze that
restores every heavy heart."

~ Torquato Tasso

The dining table is littered with the remains of our potluck dinner, plates with crumbs of almond-flour-crust pizza—my latest attempt at a no-grain/brain-healthy diet—a pot of squash soup from Dalen and Deb, some leaves of Caesar salad from Tom and Christine, plus a few bits of chocolate left in their wrappers. Our Tuesday evening ritual consists of a mad rush by everyone, coming from work and rehearsals through the icy streets of Telluride, or down from the mesa in Deb and Dalen's case, followed by the comfort of a shared meal as we sit on the sectional couch, catching up on the news of the week and laughing at Tom's jokes and impressions until we cry. Three of us five have been together since the first years of the Telluride Choral Society; Tom and Christine are welcome new additions from the past year.

My taste in music has never before stretched back to the sixteenth century, but the passions of the other four singers lean toward early music. Since they needed a fifth voice to cover the second soprano part sometimes, Peter and I welcome these dear friends into our "empty nest" in the weeks and months after Ellen's departure. I learn to float my alto/tenor voice just underneath Christine's pure soprano, moving in parallel harmony—a new incarnation of the deep and powerful voice I first discovered in the MSU Women's Glee Club thirty-five years earlier.

We are rehearsing for the Choral Society's SpringSing concerts, which are just a couple of weeks away. As we polish and refine our blend and intonation, Peter sits quietly reading in his wingback chair nearby. I hope that the harmonies and hopeful lyrics of Monteverdi's madrigal will somehow sink into Peter's brain, calming and soothing it.

His condition has still not responded, at least outwardly, to anything we have tried, and in recent months, his posture has become so stooped that he lurches forward as he walks, struggling for control as his feet shuffle clumsily along the Berber carpet. In response, I find myself calling out to him throughout the day, "Stand up straight, big steps!" This, of course, does no good whatsoever, but it is all I can do given my feelings of helplessness. One week ago, we went shopping for a walker, conforming ourselves to the inevitability. As Peter cruised through the medical supply store in Montrose with the walker, I worked hard to ignore the wheelchairs parked in the far corner. "Please, God," I prayed, "can we not go there?"

Peter's condition and the fact that I have been working solidly for the past seven months have worn me down to the point that I am questioning whether I can truly continue moving forward in all of the roles I occupy— breadwinner, wife, mother, and caretaker. It has been five years since Eliot's death and six years since Peter's symptoms first appeared. I have been moving at an unsustainable pace, and I now found myself at my very bottom—squeezed, drained, empty—with no hope in sight.

Heeding the wise counsel of a close friend, we plan a quick vacation to Cozumel immediately after my last concert of the season. The light of this counsel reaches my darkest place, and its force lifts me up enough to get through the remaining days of March, just as spring arrives. We arrive at the airport, Peter settled in a wheelchair as the airline assistant pushes him through security. Normally, I would insist that he walk, but I have no fight left in me, so I accept the help without resistance.

We have chosen Cozumel for both economic and climatic reasons. The tropical weather is a much-needed balm after a winter fraught with one snowstorm after another; I have actually developed tennis elbow from shoveling snow. And the Hotel Cozumel is having a great sale—all-inclusive/meals and room for only 122 dollars a night. This deal, paired with the miles we use toward our free airfare, fits perfectly into our budget.

Beyond the material reasons for choosing this location is a spiritual significance that became clear once we arrived. In the Mayan culture, Cozumel means "Island of the Swallows." Have you ever seen swallows fly? They can appear confused, flitting and squabbling with a fellow swallow over a few inches of real estate on a telephone line, or hundreds of them can move as one in a sweeping, grand motion across the sky—an apt reflection of humans as we walk through our lives alternating between the negative squabbles and dramas of everyday life and the positive, sublime moments when we unite and fly toward the light.

We hire a private tour guide to drive us around the island in his jeep, just to hit a few of the highlights; neither one of us is up to the rigors of an all-day group tour. We take a trip to San Gervasio, a pre-Columbia, Mayan archaeological site where Mayan women paid tribute to the goddess of love, medicine, and fertility. I walk alone through the ruins, most of them lacking the upper portions of their walls and roofs. Peter waits patiently on a wooden bench while I search for an intuition, a vision of healing. I note that all of the stone paths lead directly to the sea.

Because the tour company owner mentioned the healing waters of Punta Sur, we make that beach, located on the south tip of Cozumel, our final stop of the day. I'm not even certain he claimed the waters were healing—he spoke with a heavy accent—but in my constant focus on Peter's health, I am determined that they are, as I believe all water is healing.

Our driver, a hot, young Cozumel native—oh, how Ellen would have loved him had she been along on this trip—graciously escorts us down to the beach, guiding Peter through the obstacle course of beach chairs, tables, and umbrellas. I wait as patiently as I can for Peter to get settled, removing his shoes and shirt. I hurriedly strip off my sundress, revealing the swimsuit I had put on earlier in the day. All I want to do is to get us in the water—the "healing" water of Punta Sur.

We two swallows walk together, united, to the water's edge. It sparkles in the midday sun, clear and sharply cool as it strikes our toes. I normally will only swim in "bathtub" water, but in the name of Healing, I stride calmly forward, bracing myself to the chill, holding Peter's hand firmly until we are submerged to our bellies.

"Let me hold you," I say, wanting Peter to completely recline in the waters, to be baptized and washed clean of his illness. He nods, yielding to the moment, and allows himself—a seventy-five-year-old man—to be suspended in the crystalline water, the sun illuminating its depths while a school of angel fish swirls beneath him. I burrow my feet into the sand and lock my arms, one underneath Peter's neck and the other one, its tennis elbow straining, underneath his thighs as the waves roll in and out.

From the world of the swallows, I sing a song to the queen of the waters. I feel like I know her intimately, from the clear water of my childhood swimming pool to the Red Cedar River at MSU. From the steam of the sweat lodge and the rains of Seattle to the swift current of the San Miguel River and the sharp, cold water of Punta Sur, I call upon her to take away our sorrows, our impurities.

The song comes from my depths, each note transmitting the power of every song I have ever sung, every piece of music I have ever played, and in that moment, I know that I am composed fundamentally of song and water. My voice resonates over my husband while ripples of water play upon his chest. I feel him relax, then inhale deeply, fully. Seconds later he sobs in a rush of air as a sense of transience permeates him. "How fleeting our lives are," he will share with me later that evening. "We are all just passing through, and the present moment is precious," he will say, voice tinged with poignancy.

And then an angel fish bites him squarely on the back of his arm, a humbling reminder that we are all part of the food chain. "Let's not take ourselves too seriously," Peter would say. It is a moment of lightening up, of release. Taking the angel fish bite as our cue to exit, I release Peter from my grasp, setting his feet down in the sand, and we stagger toward the beach together.

We spend a few more days of much-needed inactivity in Cozumel. We sleep late every day, read novels by the pool, and eat at the all-you-can-eat buffet three times a day while Michael Jackson muzak blares to the far corners of the resort. My mind is quiet, blank, and at the end of the week, we take a taxi to the airport, tanned and rested. As dual airline attendants push Peter and another woman in their wheelchairs toward the gate, Peter quips a challenge, "Race you!" to the woman, a new glint in his eye.

CHAPTER THIRTY-THREE

A SHIP TURNS

One week after our return from Cozumel, following his own intuition, Peter decides to try Sinemet, the common pharmaceutical for Parkinson's disease, for the third time. Although it has previously made him ill, his worsening symptoms and our joint despair—the stem cell treatment from ten months earlier does not appear to be working—make him feel like he has no other options.

We choose a day when I can be home with him, in case he experiences any of the usual negative side effects. He takes one round, yellow pill at 9:00 a.m., sits down in his wingback chair, and waits, quietly reading. I am seated nearby on the couch, checking my email. After twenty minutes, I ask, "Do you feel anything?"

"Just a little queasy in my stomach," he responds, his hand gesticulating near his midsection. We both agree that perhaps he should have eaten something beforehand, then continue to wait. Privately, I am expecting a repeat of his two previous attempts to take this medication but keep silent and stay open to what is to come.

Forty-five minutes later, Peter gets up swiftly from his chair. Now this might not seem like a big deal, but for Peter, this simple action usually involved at least three tries, and more recently, I often have to tug him up from his chair, steadying him while he finds his balance.

"I think I'm getting out of my chair easier," he comments, looking down at his legs and feet.

I nod in agreement, a small exhale releasing from my chest as Peter sits and rises, sits and rises again—without any help.

As the slightly increased dosage—his doctor calls it a "baby dose"—circulates through Peter's system in the coming days and weeks, he begins to stride across the living room floor upright, stronger. I no longer have to call out, "Stand up straight, big steps!" because he is already doing that, without thought or effort. As his shoulders and chest open and lift, my shoulders gradually release the weight of the previous six years, my neck lengthening.

When we walk down main street in Telluride, he looks like a normal man with the exception of his left arm still slightly flagging by his side. His long legs reach farther and farther in front of him, and still, after twenty-three years of marriage, I follow them happily, my chest lifted, heart open.

CHAPTER THIRTY-FOUR

PEARLS

I n May of 2019, Ellen and I packed up all of her belongings, stuffed the car once again, and left Nashville, "Dreams" by the Cranberries blasting through the speakers.

We crooned about our lives changing every day as we coasted along the rain-soaked highway, the streetlights reflected on the road as we passed one truck after another on Interstate 40. Leaving at 9:00 p.m., our goal was to make it to West Memphis, AR so that we would at least wake up in another state. We had 1,500 miles to cover in order to be home by Mother's Day, which was only two days away; my greatest gift was to be spending so much time with my beloved daughter.

This chapter of Ellen's book was closing, for she had decided to transfer to a college just two hours away from home, Fort Lewis College in Durango. Music would always be her love, but the Environmental Studies program and the hippie lifestyle of the mountains of Colorado were calling to her.

Was this a result of Ellen's childhood in the woods, or was there some lingering residue of my earlier times in Durango passed on to her at birth? Who knew? Needless to say, we were all thrilled to be reunited with the prospect of more time together on the horizon.

The three of us flew to New Jersey in June. We were going to attend my cousin, Stefanie's, wedding, a lavish affair in mid-Manhattan. My sister, Meredith, and her husband, David, came in from Denver; they had moved there the same year I had discovered Telluride, just on the other side of the Continental Divide. We gathered at my mother's house, seated around the kitchen table, and dug into takeout from the Riviera Italian restaurant just blocks away, a favorite of my parents for the last twenty years. Three generations laughed over veal piccata and cavatelli while lightening bugs flickered in the twilight on the front lawn.

On Saturday afternoon, our high heels clacked through the house as we readied ourselves for the wedding. I appraised myself in the mirror of my parents' bedroom as I put on the string of pearls my mother had given to me thirty-two years earlier, the day that I married Eric. She re-gifted them to me today, for I had allowed her to borrow the classic strand for the past few decades as I did not have much need for such fancy jewelry in the mountains of Colorado. I feel honored, blessed, as the cool, luminescent orbs grace my neck.

Some say that pearls represent wisdom gained through experience. I hope that's true. I know that my life and its music, watered by the song of spring rivers and summer rains, has led me and mine to the heights of healing and union. That with every song I sing, I am calling to me the beauty of life, a celebration of melody and light.

That night we found ourselves reunited, joyous on the dance floor of New York City's Gotham Hall. My mother, classy in the black skirt that she used to wear when she tangoed with my father, moved to the rhythm of Rihanna's "We Found Love (in a Hopeless Place)." Meredith and David danced nearby, his hips swinging his legs comically from side to side. Ellen bounced up and down in her sparkly princess heels, her arm raised and pumping as the song's synthesizer climaxed to the chorus, her smile wide and beaming, her curls reflecting the lights from above.

And Peter and I danced energetically, throwing our arms back and sashaying our feet from side to side, sometimes grasping hands and twirling around each other, two stars in a grander orbit.

CHAPTER THIRTY-FIVE

JUNCTION CREEK

W'e've already walked about ten minutes from the trailhead as we cross the rough footbridge over Junction Creek. The water, once icy-cold from the La Plata mountains high above, warms in the June sun. On the other side of the bridge, I creep down to the creek's edge and squat, my toes just touching the water. My fingers play lightly on the surface before they anoint the top of my head, my heart, and the back of my neck.

I am cooled, redeemed.

Peter waits for me on the trail. After twenty-five years, he is accustomed to my little rituals. Maybe he is amused by them, or maybe he feels the amplification of light lifting him up as well, bubbles of grace on our skin.

We make our way along this sandy path, the first steps of the Colorado Trail, which begins in Durango. It was shown to us by our friends, Catherine and Erik, just weeks earlier, the day before we closed on our new home. We traded one small condo in Telluride for another here in Durango.

Our twenty-six-year chapter in the snowcapped mountains of Colorado near the San Miguel River has come to a close. We are ready for a new adventure, new trails to walk upon, and new scenery that doesn't constantly remind us of the losses we've sustained. It's enough that we will always carry them in our hearts, but at least we can do so while looking at a new horizon. The La Plata mountains aren't as magnificent or striking as the San Juan's. Rather, their gradual ridges are gentler, more welcoming; you don't have to have a "hard body" in order to enjoy them.

A few times a week, we enjoy this trail, only a ten-minute drive from our home. Today, after I anoint myself, we stroll up the sandy path, cobbled with large stones. I am in front, setting the pace, enjoying an unobstructed view. Junction Creek is to our left, singing a peaceful song with tones growing richer as we rise through the vegetation. My breath moves with a mantra—Ham-Sa—rhythmically every four steps.

Peter's steps are light and even behind mine. I am comforted by the sound of their ease, only gasping once in a while when Peter stretches down low and suddenly tosses a large rock aside for some extra exercise, for my ears still hold the sound of his precarious gait only a year and a half ago. I believe I will always be attuned to the stride of his long legs, in sickness and in health, as they say.

The trail rises gradually through thick vegetation that reminds me of the hillside leading up to Machu Picchu, the air sharp with a musky tang of cottonwood, oak, and ponderosa pine. A special treat in June, a proliferation of wild roses graces our path, like a housewarming gift for the spirit. Once in a while we pause for Peter to take a seat on a fallen log. While we bask in the dappled sunlight and swat the occasional mosquito, I silently compare this day to the time when Peter couldn't walk more than a city block or two without needing to stop.

The ridge rises to our left, leaving us to walk cooled in its shade as the creek winds farther from our path. The wild roses have led us to a gauntlet of sorts—a narrow trail, bordered by six-foot-tall oak bushes. Their leaves bless us on both sides, and I fan my hands through them, laughing and delighted by the sensation—Nature's car wash! Another ritual in the renewed scenery of our life.

The trail proceeds in the sunlight for a few seconds before descending into a dense thicket, and we approach my favorite part of the hike—the Enchanted Forest. Years earlier, after my family had spent that summer evening on the Fourth of July in Port Orford, OR, complete with fish and chips, we continued into northern California, pulled off the highway, and stood in the redwood forest.

"O Mitakwiyasen," I praised as I cranked my neck backward to imagine the tops of those trees. Peter took a photograph of me and Ellen at that moment. Later, we printed an eight-by-ten copy of it. Our bodies are only two inches tall. The trees, of which you can only see the very bottom, fill the remainder of the picture, their trunks easily twenty feet around. We stood, illuminated by only a few gossamer strands of sunlight that were able to penetrate the redwoods' density and form a pool around us. My face is turned upward, and Ellen's, capped by her unruly hair, was looking downward at the ferns. We are so small, indeed, in the face of Nature.

And now, in the Enchanted Forest along Junction Creek, Peter and I are embraced by the dense stand of ponderosa pines. Certainly not as glorious or awe-inspiring as the redwoods, but I feel love, and loved by them.

"Welcome home," they say, the scent of wild roses still tingeing the air. We take a break from our hike and rest on another fallen log, a smooth and comfortable bench at just the right height. After a few quiet and appreciative moments, Peter rises easily and strolls about twenty yards to a dead tree trunk that is adorned by carvings: "Sandy was here, 1977" and "Tom and Natalie, 2004."

He pulls out his Benchmade knife—the one he always has with him—and begins to carve our names into the wood, adding to a rich history. His posture is intent, leaning forward while he grips the knife with both hands, working patiently. I close my eyes and rest, the whirly song of a Swainson's thrush accompanying my daydream.

My mind dances over the details of the past fourteen months, from the time I sang in the sea of Cozumel through the wondrous months of Peter's recovery. The baby dose of Sinemet remained almost the same—just one or one and a half tablets every four hours. After two months of improvement in Peter's symptoms, we traveled to Salt Lake City to see a new neurologist—who I dubbed our "dream doctor" after our first meeting.

This was only my second trip to Salt Lake City, the first one less than a year earlier with Ellen to see Jack White.

There is a standard evaluation done on Parkinson's patients called the Unified Parkinson Disease Rating Scale (UPDRS). It is an exhaustive evaluation of a patient's mental and emotional state, physical symptoms, including gait, tremors, dexterity, speech, facial expression, bradykinesia (if any), postural stability, balance—you get the idea. Our dream doctor led Peter through all of it, taking fastidious notes and listening to every detail of Peter's health history—the supplements, the diets, the stem cells, the spiritual work, including his recent capacity to tolerate Sinemet.

Finally, he said, "You know, considering you're seventy-five years old, you are really doing pretty well. Your score on the UPDRS is a thirty-two—the higher one's score, the more advanced the disease."

We nodded, grateful for the thirty-two, for we knew that had Peter been evaluated only three months earlier—pre-Sinemet—his score would have much higher. The dream doctor made a few recommendations for us to explore, and we scheduled an appointment for another evaluation in six months.

The following January, in 2020, we again drove eight hours through the hills of Utah, winter storm clouds thickening as we climbed in altitude. Peter had kept up an exercise regimen, which included walking a half mile or more through the streets of Telluride on most days. With each easier step he took, the cloud that had taken up residence in our family lifted a bit higher, the leaden worry dissipating.

For a second time, our dream doctor evaluated every aspect of Peter's health, his face neutral during the hour-long series of tests. We talked about some blood pressure issues that Peter was experiencing, the mood casual and light. It was clear that Peter was doing better, but we were all shocked when his UPDRS score came in at a mere sixteen, down sixteen points in just six months.

When I asked the doctor what he thought could have caused this significant improvement—especially considering that Peter's medication levels remained the same—he humbly shook his head and said, "I don't know. Sometimes this just happens."

This is why I had dubbed him our "dream doctor"—he had the humility to admit that he didn't know how Peter had improved so substantially. He allowed space for the possibility that it was the stem cell treatment, or the spiritual work, or simply a "change in mood." He allowed space for the mystery of life to reveal itself, for healing to occur, and for happiness to infiltrate a typically dire situation.

When people ask my husband what he believes caused his healing, he usually responds in one of two ways.

"Faith," he sometimes answers. Not that we always had so much of it, but that we held on to that fragile blue thread, whether it was the words of José in Cusco ("He's going to improve, but not completely") or the 187 million stem cells that were harvested from Peter's fat tissue and recirculated into his brain.

Other times, Peter simply responds, "I didn't give up." That is what we can do when we don't have faith. We just keep going, one difficult step after another, one prayer after another, one tear after another.

Five months after that appointment in January is when we find ourselves in the Enchanted Forest. I open my eyes from my reverie and watch, satisfied, while Peter finishes his carving—"Peter + Rhonda" in a small heart. Our stories are joined with those of Sandy, Tom, and Natalie. I walk over and kiss him, our arms around each other, then we turn back down the trail and walk the mile home.

With a global pandemic raging around us, we decide to pass on Peter's twice-a-year evaluation in Salt Lake City that month. Instead, we continue walking, sometimes along the Animas River trail that runs through the center of Durango. At the age of seventy-six-and-a-half, Peter keeps up a good pace, but when he needs to rest, I remain upright, marching in place to keep up my heart rate. The drum cadence of the "The Series" still rings in my ears, and I swing my arms from side to side, my imaginary saxophone digging into my ribs. He doesn't always feel so great—his shoulders ache from past injuries, and his energy wavers—but I remind him that he is getting older, after all.

We delay our trip to Salt Lake City for another five months, finally squeezing it in November, before the pandemic gets even more out of control. The same tests of Peter's mental acuity, memory, and physical symptoms take place while we chat about the weather and the state of health in the big city. Our dream doctor's assistant takes a few moments to tabulate the results of the lengthy exam, and we wait, hoping that if Peter has slipped some, it's not too much.

"Well," she pronounces, peering over her computer. "Looks good—your score today is a five."

I start laughing bubbles of wonder and glee and turn towards Peter, the new number and its vibration just sinking in with him. Moments later, as we check out of the clinic, all we can do is smile, shaking our heads. I keep calling him "Mister Five" as we glide to our car, allowing ourselves to be carried on a new current.

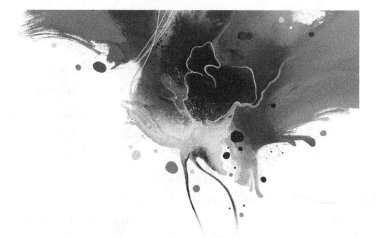

CHAPTER THIRTY-SIX

A STREAM OF SONG

T he musicians, masked, enter the Veterans of Foreign Wars (VFW) hall with instruments in hand. They obediently line up to have their temperatures taken, a miniscule inconvenience outweighed by the anticipation and joy of seeing friends for the first time in four months.

Four flutes, three clarinets, one bass clarinet, one alto sax, two trumpets, one horn, one trombone, one euphonium, one tuba, and two percussionists—a skeletal concert band by most standards, but quite perfect for the first movement of Gustav Holst's "First Suite" in E-flat. Holst himself said that the arrangement should allow for only nineteen players, plus percussionists, to perform it. In this time of a global pandemic, the Southwest Civic Winds board approved a band of seventeen, plus a handful of board members, to participate in my audition process.

We had scheduled an outdoor rehearsal, but Nature had other plans. The summer monsoon pattern had started, so it was quickly decided that we move the audition indoors. I couldn't be more grateful, for the acoustics inside would be much more forgiving than the outdoors. The wind, whipped up, would have blown away everyone's music and sound, scattering fragments above Durango.

The musicians sit a safe distance from each other, seven to nine feet between rows, taking up the entire dance floor. It's awkward to have so much space between us—musicians are accustomed to working side by side, hearing those close to us breathing, fingering through technical passages, keys clacking in preparation for the actual moment, an intimate experience. Socially distanced, we are subject to feeling isolated, vulnerable, our weaknesses exposed—much like many of us have felt during the last four months of sheltering-in-place.

Once everyone is seated, we remove our masks and the comforting sound of scales and long-tones fills the room. I am standing at the front, glancing through my score, breathing deeply in an effort to calm myself. Though I am the only person invited to audition for the position of Artistic Director, I am aware of the technical prowess of this group. "Please God," I pray, "let me know now if I'm not good enough for this job. I don't want to fake my way through this." I decide I'll just do the best that I can.

After a few scales together, we play a short chorale—Frank Erickson's "Air for Band"—to get used to the strange acoustics of being socially distanced. We learn together the necessity of watching my baton, rather than listening to each other, in order to stay together rhythmically. The increased distance combined with the live acoustics of the hall creates a great lag from back to front, and I work hard to transmit the ictus more clearly to the percussionists who stand like masked, yet eager, sentinels.

Even though we are not quite synced, I allow the group to play all the way through "Air for Band." Perhaps the board members who are watching on the sidelines wonder why I don't stop to correct the diminishing tempo, but I don't have the heart to do so. These players, me included, haven't played "live" with others for four months—quite likely the longest period of time any of us have ever gone without since before we were kids in our school band programs.

After the final cymbal crash of the piece, I allow a moment for the sound to circulate through the hall before I drop my arms. This is the "magical moment" I used to teach my middle school band students about, when the final vibrations are still reaching the audience members. "Don't move!" I would admonish them, "The audience is still experiencing your sound, and we don't want to distract them with our horns flashing down to our laps."

Finally, I release my arms—and the players. I take a deep inhale and scan facial expressions across the room. A reverent silence settles upon us, while our cells and neurological pathways awaken after a long season's nap. One of the flute players has a dreamy look on her face, tears in her eyes.

"How did that feel?" I ask them. They nod quietly. No words can describe the taste and sound of water after months in the desert.

I chose Holst's "Suite" in E-flat for the main part of the audition to attend to all of our comfort levels. Every concert band musician knows this piece inside and out; I knew these folks would be able to execute their parts well enough so that its spirit would come through.

I raise my arms and give two preparatory beats to indicate the tempo. The tuba and euphonium enter from across the ballroom, and it is no longer me conducting but Mr. Morgan in a late winter rehearsal in the Clifton High School band room. I can smell the leather music folders, the stuffiness of the damp room, and the scent of valve oil as the opening melody joins the present with the past, just a blink of forty years in the span of a few seconds.

With the ensuing trumpet entrance, then the clarinets, I am in Vassar. I see my student, Tanya, lean into her entrance, her eyes glowing, surrounded by her bandmates, clad in flannel on an early February morning, the roads outside slick with another eight inches of wet snow and ice. The clarinets sing me into the Evergreen Junior High School band room, where I sit in the flute section of the Washington Wind Symphony. We pick up the dance of eighth and sixteenth notes, a reflection of the rain that spatters on the roof on a dark Monday evening.

The stream of song gathers me southward, from the Pacific Northwest to the snowcapped mountains of Colorado, where half of the rehearsals of the Telluride Wind Ensemble have been decimated during a god-awful February flu season. We reunite at the final dress rehearsal and sink into the comfort of Holst, the flute and oboe solos sweet, until the music propels us onward, the melody in inversion, the point of no return.

As we launch toward the final statements of the main theme, I am spun forward another sixteen years into 2018, to my beloved Telluride students, many of whom I initiated into the concert band world as sixth graders. They play the Holst "Suite" at their final high-school band concert, dedicating it to me, for I was leaving the public schools, finally allowing myself to "graduate" along with my daughter. In their enthusiasm and love, the kids rush toward the ending, their hearts leaping forward with such energy that I find myself landed two years later in this present moment, settling into my black boots with a slight rebound in front of the Southwest Civic Winds.

We reach the last few measures, punctuated by the greatest bass drum strikes in all of history. I fling my arms to the back of the room, smiling broadly, unmasked, and the percussionist's eyes gleam back at me. The final E-flat major chord fills the hall, and the high "C" of the trumpet reverberates for seconds after the release.

I drop my arms, nod, and say, "Let's continue."

FINE—THE END

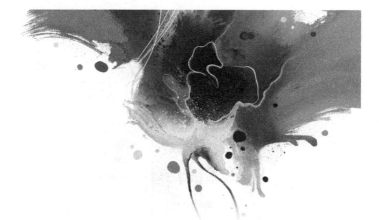

ABOUT THE AUTHOR

R honda L. Muckerman is an accomplished music teacher and conductor. For over thirty-five years, she has taught musicians of all ages and is currently the Artistic Director of the Southwest Civic Winds and Assistant Artistic Director of the Durango Choral Society. She lives in Durango, Colorado in the San Juan mountains, near the Animas River with her husband, Peter.

Find out more about Rhonda's work at
rhondalmuckerman.com

A free ebook edition is available with the purchase of this book.

To claim your free ebook edition:

1. Visit MorganJamesBOGO.com
2. Sign your name CLEARLY in the space
3. Complete the form and submit a photo of the entire copyright page
4. You or your friend can download the ebook to your preferred device

Print & Digital Together Forever.

Snap a photo

Free ebook

Read anywhere